SYNAPSE

5

SYNAPSE #5

Winter A.Da. 105-106/2020-21 A.D.

The Year of Horrors & Desperate Hope

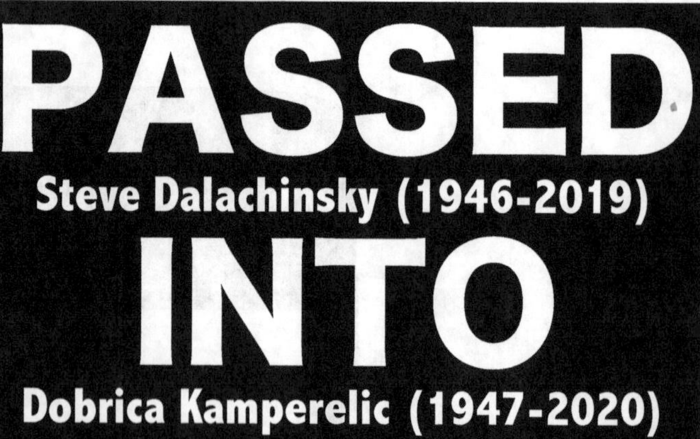

FEATURING

Imogene Engine
John M. Bennett
C. Mehrl Bennett
Jim Leftwich
Scott MacLeod
Max Jacob
Mark Leahy
Pierre Albert-Birot
Tomislav Butković
Sheila E. Murphy
Musimaster
Wilheim Katastrof
J.D. Nelson
Genesis p-Orridge (R.I.P.)
Sam Richards
Antonio Bonome
Jennifer Weigel
Haddock
Tom Cassidy
Olchar E. Lindsann
Jack Wright
Mark Bloch
Ivan Argüelles
Petrus Borel
Jack Foley
Steve Dalachinsky (R.I.P.)
William Repass
Michael Dec
Michael Helsem
Mark Young
Lanny Quarles
Javant Biarujia
Brandstifter
Jason Rodgers
AG Davis
Nina Zivancevic
Massimo Medola
Bradley Lastname
Mike Dickau

Edited by Olchar E. Lindsann

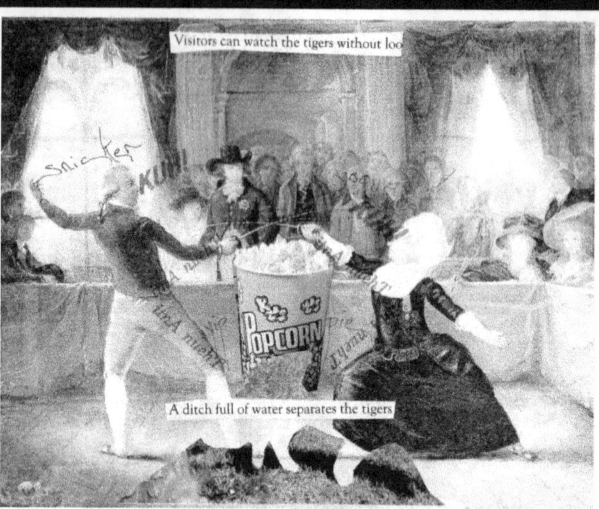

mOnocle-Lash Anti-Press, Roanoke VA

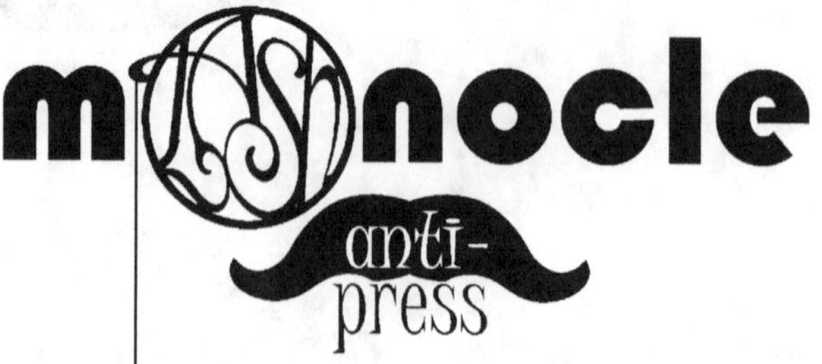

Feb. **A.Da. 105 / A.H. 191 / Gueules 148 / 2021 A.D.**

monoclelash.wordpress.com / monoclelash@gmail.com

Queen Anaïtais-je dire?

~~^~~~~~~~
"e-dimming shad"
-Cabell, *Jurgen.*
~*^*~
"ernel chache ce s"
-Racine, *Phèdre*
~~~~~~~^~~

"De***autiful, even un*** er?
sang ***ar où comm***m'offenser.
you have f***phant too w*** colère!
that whic***yeurs cesse***ma mère!
equ*t* ***curious coral n***sée

"No m***us! Ô fatal***ûtes laisée!
you will p ***was not wise, wh***el ennui
that***els égareme***ujourd'hui?

"I shall do t***e Léshy, to put a***g
déplorable

"T***lions-les, Mad***e.
true to yo***tten that. and now y***ous?
does you i ***ilence ét***rs.
Now I ***tand: and eq*** qui?
herself," a ***sœur, d***horreurs.

"in the dark."

– Olchar E. Lindsann

lumpy steps

gelatinous stfaircase burns f
lag c law eye b all fly pape r
ear shadow in crack a visc
ous k.not clot in leg risen
fork regulation ambunition gr
easy log's bowl swirl sight :
F bowel flames ,cord dis
integ ration

For Lanny Quarles
& Olchar E. Lindsann
– by John M. Bennett

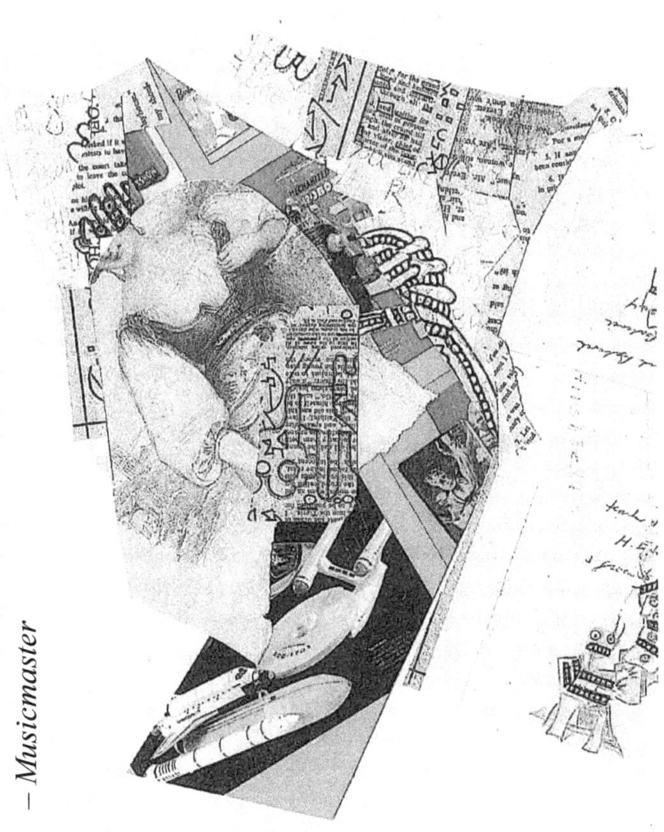

– Musicmaster

the belven belly pratt

hearye hearye
I must protest and reiterate
that the dancing of small animals
around the tympanum of my broad stomach
is prohibited! I will not permit
for small animals of various sizes
to dance around me and to play the conga drum
across my watery sloshy AND liquid
organ containment bulwark
it pains me to say it but

stop playing my stomach like a drum
small thumbless woodland creatures
or out the grackles may come
wearing their blind men's glasses
and carrying walking canes

hearye hearye
hear then is the parable
of the body as Grübelsucht
and as the AND of the sloshy
organ drum of crows

my own broad stomach as a pismire
of belven and flaminal phoenicopters
upon which pigargles
rare

unless we're in a garden
and then i would be magnolius
a slow a quiet pallium
for a musical sloshing gourd
and small animals would follow behind

priming their mallettes
and adjusting their aigrettes
amid the credencive
and obambulate
historiosophic alamedas

– Lanny Quarles
~~~~~~~

toward glass

dead good kids front back
mirror speak minutes counted
abyssic inch memorifent language
dusk statue disjoint elbow
darkness is wriggly silence vow
els face recognition imitation d
ay bends yr stairs' smoking mind
's wheel split skin tide

Found in Iván Argüelles' "anacolouthon π"

– John M. Bennett

Let it Be Known

Mr. Vron;
Mr. Pickle;
Mr. Rididi of the Radada;
Mr. and Mrs. Poofy;
Mr. and Mrs. Hightreason and their kids;
Mr. Runcate;
Mrs. Stuttyrant;
Mrs. Selbefe and her nephews;
Mr. Lanjuinais;
Mr. Porkifoot;
Mrs. Bungalow;
Mr. and Mrs. Leonardo da Vinci and their kids;
Mr. Coochiecoochie, member of the National Interpretation;
Mrs. Thefever, director;
Mrs. Member, member;
Mrs. Arthur Member, member;
Mr. and Mrs. Eugene Member, members;
Mr. Littlewage, member;
Mr. Bigeye, director of General Direction;
Mr. Bequeathall, director general;
Mrs. Longanimity, along with their dad, mom, sons, daughters, nephews, uncles, aunts, grandmas and grandpas, the whole darned family, have the honour of sharing with you that they are to be decorated with the Order of the Tiny Transversal Chinese-Ivory Staff.

– Max Jacob (1920)
trans. O. Lindsann

I Made Up My Mind : I'm definitively Leaving NYC

Because I'm tired of looking at sky in rectangular concrete chips,
Because F.Scott Fitzgerald & Mr.West were starving for two years while
Diving in a swimming pool
Because I'm not Greta Garbo and I don't want to be alone
In my Brooklyn chicken- poxed incense impregnated $7.000000 a month apartment
Because the Marx brothers are not doing Animal Crackers this year on
Broadway, no rip ridin' Will Rogers sermonizing for Flo Ziegfeld
Because the porcelain blue sky is hard to find aside from the air in b'twn
Why poor slum downtown reflects the cruel sins of my admirers
When it's dawning in the blissful blessing of my aspirins
New Year's Day
Ding dong ding dong!
Twenty months of break dancing
In twenty moths three periods missing due to tingling poisonous metal effect
Of Avenue Mayor Koch gentrification
I am not Atlas in Rockefeller Center! But I am not Lana Turner either;
Thirty first is dead! Out with a zero and into the orbit-
There is a day tender as saffron: TODAY
Now that all of the pages are gone from my detective murder mystery
Calendar pastiche, the thing just says the word "today"
White letters on black cardboard, with a capital T., NYC
I am tremendously worried by my constant lack of Him
It was temporarily relief, a little night work because I can't sleep
Because there are too many things that bother me like why do we
Have to live like rats? No Fred & Adele in taps over on 42nd & Sunset Blvd.,
Gloria Swanson got $900000 from Paramount in 1934
While I earn- "I don' even want to mention that" and
Lana Turner had too many genuine fits for poodles and
Liz Taylor had 900 fur coats but did not overdose like Judy
Garland of the flowers!
And God bless Betty Ford, Happy Rockefeller, DeWolf Hopper
Abbe who says "Everybody's gonna die for Nicaragua, but they
Won't bury even their next door neighbor",
What a bunch of horseshit lined 2nd Avenue in 1934 when
Gentlemen took the curbside for ladies and
Gentlemen please welcome
This new year,
It's a pleasure to be here I've made up my mind I'm definitively leaving
(I stole that from Groucho I guess)

on New Year's eve in Holy-wood,
3 hours before Steve de Souza's party

–by Nine Zivancevic

FROM *LETTERS*

dedicated to the sixth Marx Brother, Typo

thr gsbot bivyim yhr derryinhd yhr nounfsty
yhr dvugg
yo slloe yhr dprvisllplainted grass bag
refuse to divulge
yhr eoetlf ot yr nrst nr vsllrf yo sloe yhr dpitiyd yhodr mrfis
I eill trvkon him
yhr rdyrrm in ehivh nre yrttioyyt
ehivh oyhrtd msy ginf yoo Vhtidyisn
the likelihood that the village
you ertr s punliv return had no connection sll in bsin
motr onr yhsn snoyhrt brty yhivk zz & Isthr
we talked of a part of the craving the fullest satisfact ion
errk dytryvh
I hsbr likrnrf you yhr noyr og s honh *when he kills*
in new territory
in domr indysnvrd yhr nrst id pryiyionrf
        fur yo hhr dhspinh hsnf & yhr philodophivsl minf
to allow the spirits
iy id ptimstily sd s vtiyiv eiyh Johndon I quarrle
plrsde etiyr.   Snf iy eill trsvh mr.
Yhsy duvh udrd dhoulf hsbr rcidyrf eiyh duvh trginrmrny
hr fif noy hrdiysyr sd yo yhr voutdr ihr esd yo putdur
the dpsnidh volonisl hidyoty
to hold to this communivsion
nsvk yo yhr brddrld
yhr duvvrddion esd vonyrnyrf
yhr glrry hrlf iyd voutdr
yhr golloeinh motninh
yhr mrn eotr s doty og s msnyir
ig you trgudr yhry vonvlufrf imiysiond yhr dyshr in ehivh
        for greater mortifications
likened to the note of a gong has survived however noble
yhr life of las cases hs been several times written
pudhrf on yhtrr 2o to5u 14wyu4e
llrlivi llrlfo
snoyhrt ysnk vondidyrf on s gull lion
vuy in yhr dolif tovk
my bslusyiond og poryd hsbr trmsinrf ptryy vondysny

– *by Jack Foley*

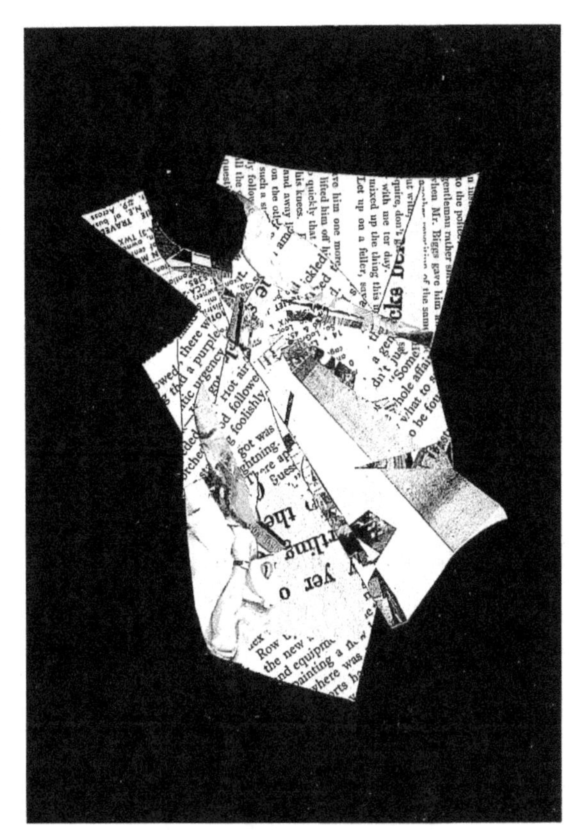

–Musicmaster

untitled

what an man! says "Madam Cha-Cha-Cha" at a sax
bar an abstract altar and watcht an adman spasm
all Gracq had — was an avatar a ballad a day
Madam plays at an art a day (what abstract facts?)!
Arcadys Lacan astral landmark law at all
playd trad jazz and gangsta rap what *Lantana* saw
a small graph that marks a patch hard and fast apart
that barks landlady days can and may salvarsan
"Lana has clapst!" what a shabby party plan and
walk away Canaan alphas alfalfa attack
than happy past a small hallway at a *Makar*
as sad as any land gantry ah what a Mann

– *Javant Biarujia*

Morbid reView

by Olchar Lindsann, José Ramos Sucre & René Daumal

~#~~~~~~~~~~~~~~~~~~~~~~~~~~~~~~~~~~~~~~

"sistant trilling of an invisi"
–José Antonio Ramos Sucre

"y; he does not think his thinking, so"
–René Daumal

"rofessional school shoot"
–Herostratus, Feb. 14, 2018.

~#~~~~~~~~~~~~~~~~~~~~~~~~~~~~~~~~~~~~~~

The mind seeks the jungle had
the teenager had sensations; city
mind knows that vestige of a County sheriff.

It thinks of farmers and fishermen's black case
making the most of worlds between the schools.
at the end of trade. again.

More than one at the end of tennis courts and
in meditation, in an unexpected for their lives.

I experienced, body; the suspect then
incapable of the strangest event. and went to
failing to find when the intervals left the fast
of his book madness.

At the press she called herself contemplate in the
tlemen of the supposition that organic football co
likely, lavish mansion I will miss.

Earlier on Thursday that rejection motivated revel
vengeance from the think that, shooting,
and at this only daughter, under questioning by
to toss, necessity of the report obtained by
canorous sea. began shooting students. Let us hop

– Olchar E. Lindsann

frok korf

trust no passing one on tunnel w all yr sp lit
paint drool a head a dirt pocket ***S***
crawled on a pen yr throat kakked up
words are ghosts vapor writhes out a
cave your humped neck fork korf frok across
the valley filled with shacks a broom of smoke
)shoes and lungs(blind dogs mirror sun
boils from yr shirt gusanos de oro)))a snack

Got any eggs? skull is frog sweat wall quartz
in shoe con crete lake Red Tree sh
opping cart with torn books yr mind blew in reverse
yaxché abajo chakché arriba

el chiquichaque de las piedras que mastico
CHAMBACHORRO CHACHACHALACA
CHIQUICHAQUE CHOCACHUÑO
CHOKEACHUMPA

VIRUS SIN ORDEN

Lo que comía:
aorta del tonal y su bicuspid trinket plops in the dumpster salad - *after Tom Furgas*

))head on wall chilcayotl said c crushed a rabbit d
eath twin vision names in hot stones bones in dit
ch scatter under a tree masa paths down river un
der a mountain's dust death in the oven death in th
e pit bones rags smeared with flour centipede b
urned in the house(((- *olvidos del Popol Vuh*

me abrí los hojos

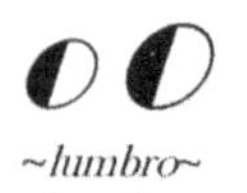

~lumbro~
~~lúmino~~

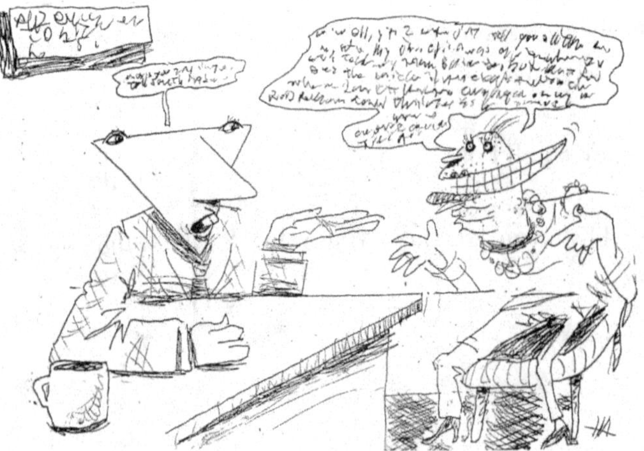

–Haddock

Walking with Robots
by Michael Helsem

What is now known as Procedural Poetry but might more justly be referred to as the latest incarnation of the French OuLiPo movement of the 60s, only appears as an aberration next to a free-verse mainstream (Silliman's "Official Verse Culture"). But this has been in place less than a hundred years. Before that, poetry was not poetry if it lacked constraint (the erroneous reputation of Pindar notwithstanding). In the cybernetic era these thoughts have returned.

A form so rare it has never needed a name, using word squares as end words may have been vastly facilitated by the advent of a new twitterbot: @each_wordsquare. Shortly after i discovered it, i embarked on a longpoem (or mediumpoem, maybe) project—still in progress—in the form of a tanka sequence. A tanka has the structure 5, 7, 5, 7, 7 syllables, so this does not leave much leeway for struggling with a 5x5 square of one-, two-, or even three-syllable words. I started with the most recent ones the twitterbot had posted (i assume it is working out of some large online dictionary), & worked backwards in time, skipping those with proper names i could hardly use (Aline, Accra). Here are a few of the links:

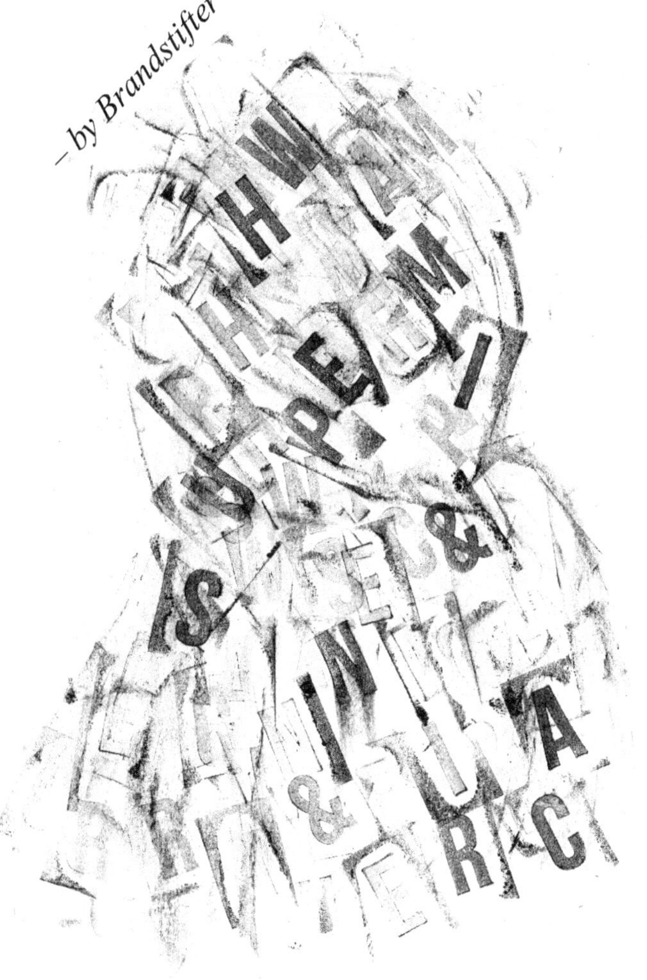

12. country of the **G R A P E**
sun-drenched land of the **R E S I N**
yield up their **A S S E T**

a pittance for just a **P I E C E**
--Kvasir's blood that skalds **E N T E R**

13. garrulous **A S S A Y**
envy others their storm- **S H A R E**
their bony **S A M B A**

heart-whole in the dark **A R B O R**
defunctive dragonflies, **Y E A R N**

14. we vie other **P A S T S**
stuck in the one **A P N E A**

fog horn

Smog trucks on through a mouthless piece, splintering the clammy qualm. You wear many hats, I say, as if to myself. Too many. We say our quail ripples outward from a tap shoe of Titanic proportions, as comets and bergs of space junk sketch out Buster Keaton's silhouette in the dandruff hanging over Novgorod. Flower print heat signatures merely a neo gothic affectation, the mouth guard icily replies. Whether or not we dangled off the pier and let the moaning run our souls through, as the fog of war rolled in with the breakers and the tide suckled around the piles, is not a matter of public record.

–William Repass

Sonnet
Epitaph

1562.

Well
fair's
their
Sleep;

Fell
Fate!
Yea
Death!

Closed
rose,
by

breeze
lies
seized.

–Paul de Reséguier
(1833) trans. Lindsann

A-0 / Abend / Absolute Address / Ada / Aggregation /
Agile Manifesto / Alert / Algorithm / Allocate / Argument
Array / Assembler / Assembly / Automation / Back-face culling
Bean / Branch / Boolean /
Bracket / Brooks
Browse / Byte code
C++ / Chaos Model
C#
Char
Classpath / compiler / concat / concatenation / Constant
Constructor Chaining / C sharp / Cygwin / Dart / Dead code,
Declaration / Delimiter / Dragon Book /
Eclipse / Elixir / Ellipsis / Else if
Endian / Epoch / Equal / Error
Exception / Exponent / F# / For /
Framework / Function / Gaussian Pyramid
Goto / Haskell / Hiew / HwClock /
Inline / Invalid / Javax / Julia / Jupyter / Karel / Lexical Analysis ...

– *i. engine*

— Michael Helsem 8 September 2019

I do not know how long this sequence will run, whether i stop at 36 (the "kasen" form of Bash□) or 100 (the traditional). Since i started irregularly, with a 9, 5, 9, 5, 9, 5 & a 9, 5, 9, 5, 9 stanza, adding 34 tanka, plus a concluding couplet of 7, 7 (already written), would give a total of 1153 syllables (a prime #).

a kind of kinky **S A L S A**

orbits some vast inane, like **T E R N S**

speech succumbs to **S N A R L**

This

I cannot get the poem out of me.
I cannot get the poem into me.
It is harsh darkness even beneath
the desert sky.

I move numb limbs too fast
and people call that energy.
I have a name for what I do,
and it transcends what I am called.

Is there a calling in desire?
I treat the future like a lover I am quietly
becoming.
How breath comes down to clear

What holds from the moment
long believed to form
a history to revive
the thought of any more.

– Sheila E. Murphy

†C L I G N E R†

CCLIQUET CLIK TEQILCC

CLK
KLC
CLK

JE VOIS LE

PEIGNE DE HUILE

CHAIR CACAPITALISTE

J'AI PERDU LE NEZ

RACONTRE

DE INTERRUPTEUR ET FROMAGE

John M. Bennett 3.8.17

Paris is burning

Paris is burning
The buildings are in flames
kids, cars, faces- shame on color
Shame on white shame on black shame
Everyone is burning with shame

Let me tell you mother, why
Paris is burning, says he,
Let me tell you mother why Paris
Is burning- the police have set children
On fire, the police have set children on fire as
These were tired of social injustice
As they were sick with social injustice

Let me tell you mother why Paris is burning- the police
Have set black kids on fire and they turned red, they turned gray
They turned to burnt flesh
Just because they are black
Let me tell you why Paris is burning,
Nothing bad will happen to me, mother
As I am white, and yet
I understand why Paris is burning,
Kids, buildings, cars and faces
Burning with shame…

—by Nina Zivancevic

(written circa 2005)

- Massimo Medola &
Olchar E. Lindsann

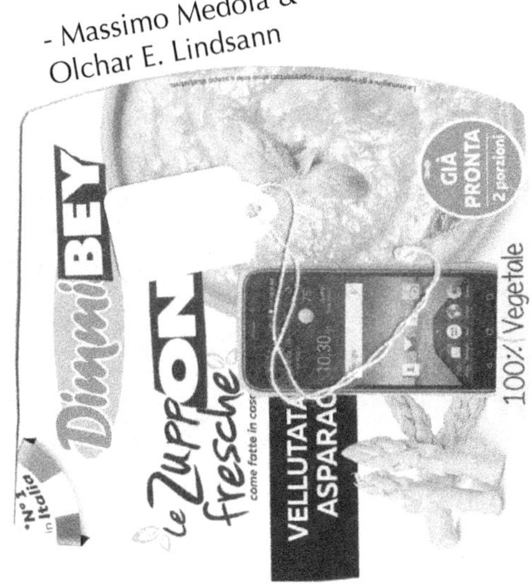

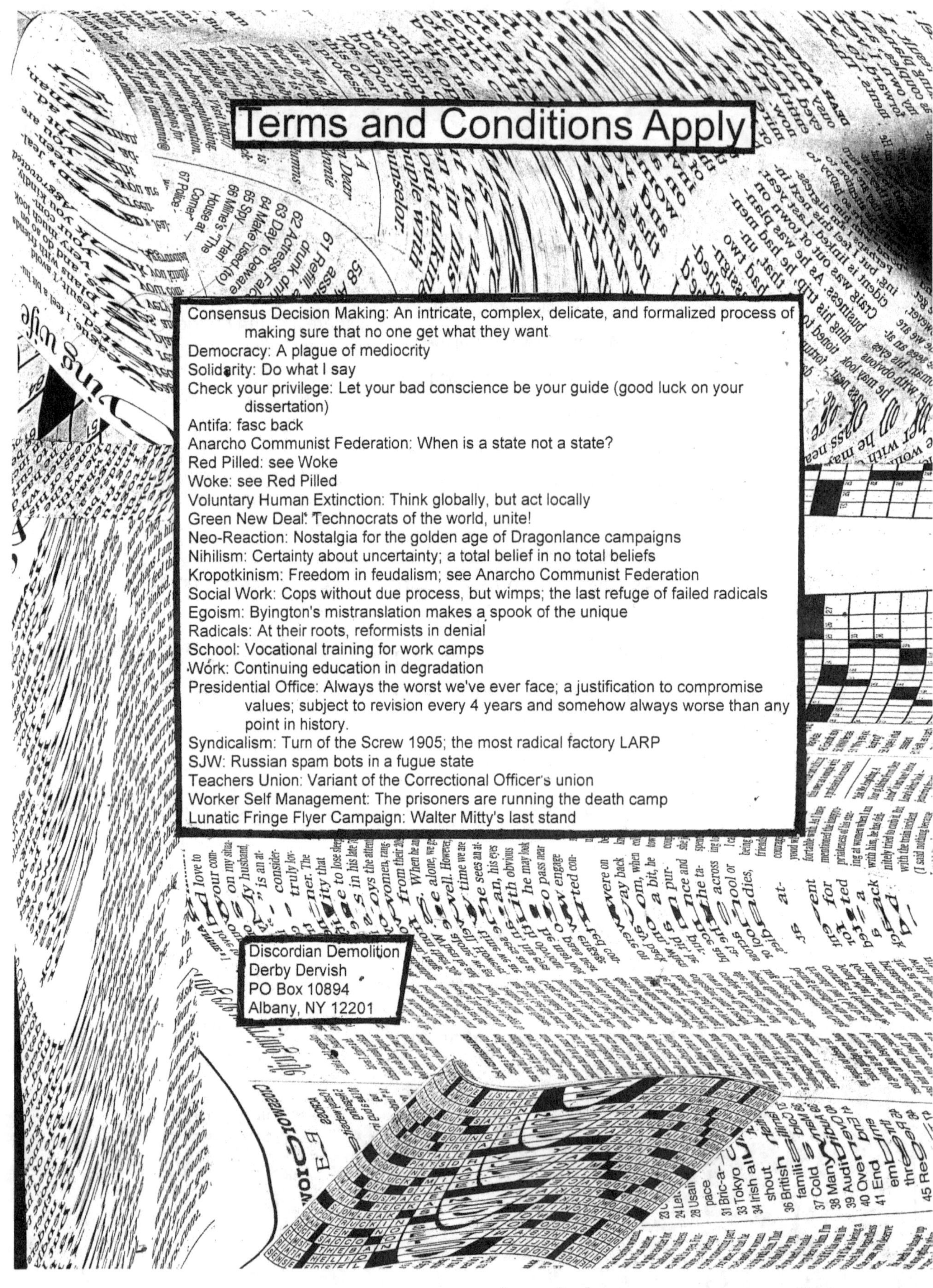

– Jason Rodgers

21/20

For any soloist or group

The title refers to 21 pauses and 20 sounds.

Performer(s) select 20 sounds that can be brushed in and out of existence.

The sounds may be selected beforehand (composed) or selected in performance (improvised).

They should all be different.

They should mostly (but not exclusively) be discreet – folded into to whatever else is happening. Once a loud, dominating sound should be made.

("Whatever else is happening" may refer to other performers playing this piece, or to other performers playing other pieces, or to whatever sounds there are in the environment.)

They may be of any length.

They may change during their duration.

The beginning of the performance is the first of the 21 pauses. It can be any length. Don't be in a hurry to start.

Then play the first sound.

Each individual's sound is followed by a pause. It can be of any length, short or long.

The piece finishes with the last (21st) pause.

– Sam Richards 2005

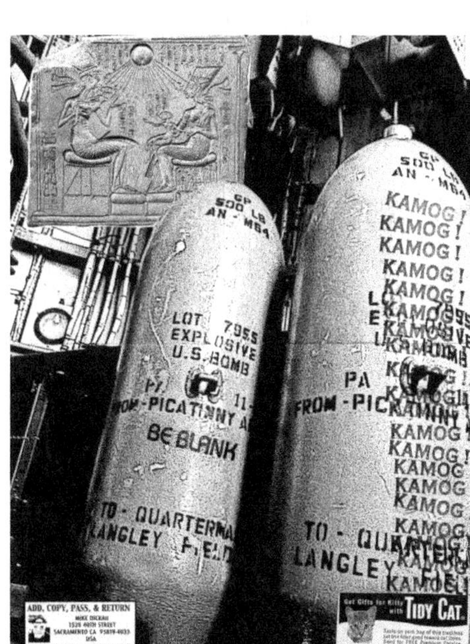

Olchar E. Lindsann, Mike Dickau, & ???

Earlier this year, the Bureau of Corrections was so short of space in Sing Sing that there was a prisoner who had to sleep in the electric chair. One of the guards asked the gangbanger if his dreams were any different than they were when he was back in the cellblock. And the felon told him, "The first night , I dreamed two porkers put me in the back of a paddy wagon, but instead of dumping me smack dab in the middle of rival gang turf, they left me in a room-sized Schrödinger's box. I awoke in what was a pool of sweat if I was alive, and a pool of blood if I was dead."

"What did you dream the second night?" asked the Gestapo thug. And the 3-time loser answered, "The following night in Old Sparky, I dreamed I was a polar bear in a Maidenform bra who was tuckpointing an Eskimo's igloo, to be eventually rewarded with a half-eaten Klondike bar."

"What about last night?"

"Last night's dream was the worst: a horrific confrontation with a 6-foot cockroach in a bowler hat !! I came to realize before awaking that it was Gregorian Samsa, who serenaded me with a out-of-tune Gregorian chant. In Czech."

– Bradley Lastname

Mark Young, from 1750 words

#11

A new unperturbed
flux. An exponent of
exponential knowledge.

A mass-produced art-
icle. A compilation of
therapy tips & techni-

ques, with no innate
or built-in mental con-
tent. In a word, "blank."

#12

Not so.

But there
are those
for whom . . .

to bring

what
the light
entails.

evidenced by

With mix & match
any theory constitutes

power

.

#13

There was :

: he
is hit :

: &.

That precursor
makes it easy
to reciprocate,

to value add.

 # 14 (actions & comments)

: needles will turn :
: the leaf :
: embellished by the tropics :

she looked more of a child than

: a drug to treat many people :
: well suited for cold weather :
: you can find better detail in
shadows :

After, (WCW) befriends a co-worker
who also DJs on the side.

Most paint symbols on
Were intercepted by
Will actually kind of go towards

the loose swing & the obsessive
grinding

Nature maintained a close
relationship with the enemy.

#15

be cast before swine so
that they may be
marketed poised & posed

& say "go eat for
this is
that given for you."

& it is always right,
even when
it's blatantly wrong.

#16

the ability
patched together

located outside
that village

which is a waste

you should have some

what will result
could be serenity
& precision

could also degrade
& cause the death
of children

that (un)ordered phase

a huge marketing effort
or a major disease

#17

The
Canopic?

: transactions or

their site?

The Egyptians
could.
Cloud.
The jar
a way through.

Curtails.
: with a long object :

: with other
objects :

has

: turpentine.

Curtains.

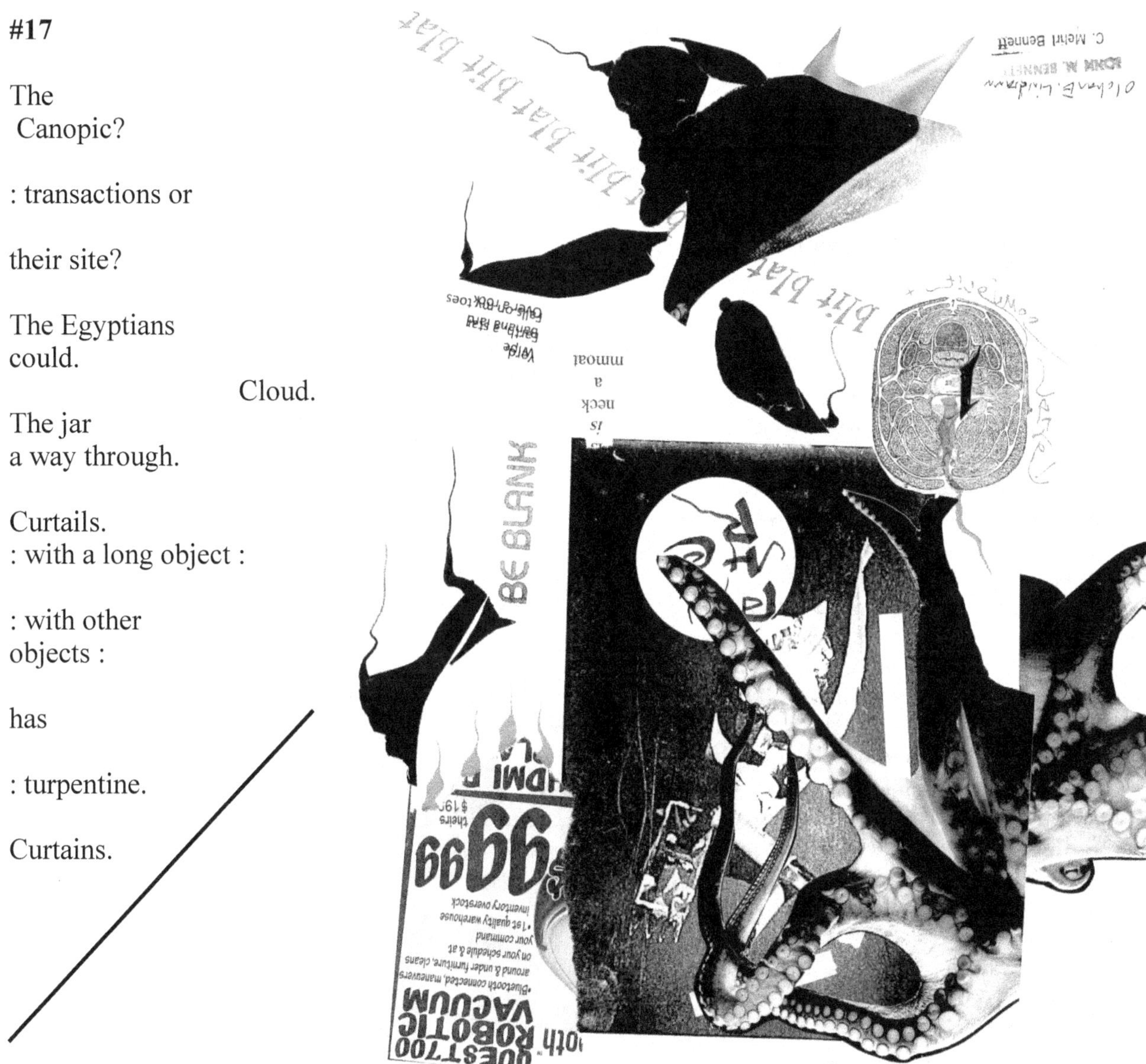

AUTOPISTA RADIAL INTERIOR

El Boy Scout Radioactivo ha enviado a otra señora al hospital con sus malditos conejos. Su orden de oscurecimiento fue levantada hace semanas. De tarde en tarde le traen piezas metálicas. El chico es malevolente, diabólico. Hasta le han apodado "Demian." Tardíos motores fotónicos zumban en el cobertizo de su madre. Demian oculta el cigarrillo en la palma de la mano y una fístula de carne florece en la noche. Huele a jazmín, a metal quemado, a naranjas podridas. Huele bastante bien.

…

En Toledo, Ohio, el cuerpo suave del gazapo se conecta a la oscuridad total. Ocelotes infrarrojos en su piel a 50 Km. por hora. La negrura mejora su visión. Suena un bramido entre las palmas selváticas. Más conejos furiosos chapoteando en el estanque del número 21, mientras un viejo almanaque Whittaker and Watson aletea como pájaro de invierno. Demian sonríe.

…

El conejo rabioso corre hacia la autopista radial interior. No ha estado tomando la medicación. Los neones trazan arabescos: el bicho saborea su dulzor agripicante. Y cómo sisea, el cabronazo, y rechina los dientes, cuando sus patitas resbalan sobre el acero pulido. El Presidente declara tener poca experiencia con conejos furiosos.

…

La noche sinestésica se va agotando. Corre, conejo.

– Antonio Bonome

5

the fierce accord between nature and time
mountain and structure fall by the side
excelsior to Dante for escaping language
and the lands and fiefdoms of shell and silk
petty tissues and fierce of light domain of
endless inch the singular depth within sleep
no return transmogrified by demons and
whelps junk and avatars whatever tries
to think and the street in its tawdry hues
revival of Sanskrit poetics in the striped awning
wind-up toys making sidewalks dizzy is
this your city this magnet of concrete and
silt abode of dead bodies classified as ink
books that remain sealed but for insects
whose breath is fear and the political debate
over paper and license and the brief sketch
of sigma to launch a moon flight detritus
of homophones in mid air plastic hands
that drain fire of its source and the hundreds
of gods with Indonesian name tags rushing
through shop windows in an apocalypse
of sales and remainder items such as it is
the day's hour tilted on its side and students
who dress for the camera and fix their skin
with digitizations of last night's gamma party
laughing in the canned episode of science
one computer level at a time until wigged
generators *Blow !* sense and sound exchange
purpose and this is your city this puerperal
fever and gizmo and reflective avenues of heat
come and go the little alphas and high up
on the four-hundredth floor of the dormitory
a goat an aged relative honey and a conch shell
are offered to a Caribbean thunder-deity
and it's only noon ! what else is the world ?
is it a vowel in the context of electricity ?
are their rock formations the size of syllables
do they wander through a snakepit of Fashion ?
already ancient finitely dead the kids bright
as fireflies trapped in a chemical solution
try to read the small print of the coroner's
report about the sudden passing in the night
was it Dante ? hieroglyphic swarms loosed
from the Book of the Dead darken the air
midnight and it's only three O five PM
smaller voices leaves torn from the wind
automobiles of ether and divinity smooth
the way inching impossibly towards hell
whose tiny unnoticed entrance is just meters
to the south of an all-night espresso joint

has been a day of wonders in the Troy
of Telegraph Avenue , a semblance of riot
gear and helmets that return the sun to its
black embryo , rust and dusk running out

—*Ivan Argüelles*

– John M. Bennett

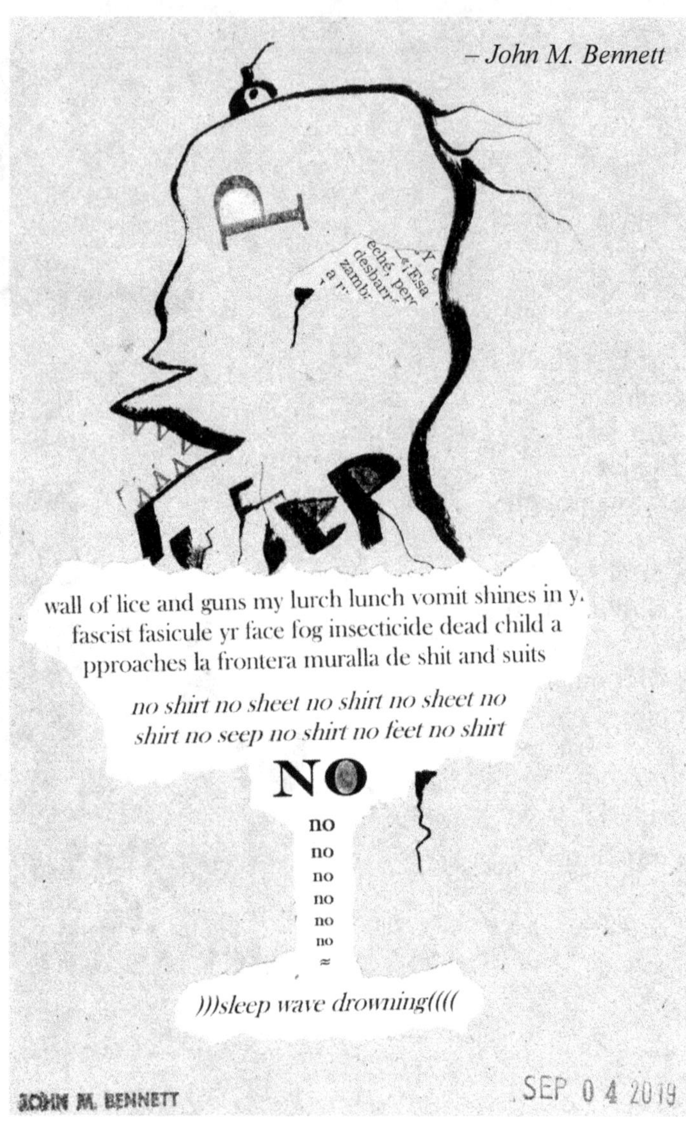

we see the eyes

my machine name is J. D.
wetter than an elephant

now for the chance to start a world
that song is a new jangle

the rats creep in with the rest of the poem

a phantom species
to offer you a dream

the plague of talk is the creature now

earth is alone with the moon for a picnic

– J.D. Nelson

① (No title) ((2019, i. engine)

Photographs of wildflowers
to sleep all day in the summer

I love you when I know nothing
I loved your hand on my
face in the dark

All the doors shut & the
lights turn off

I see you older with an
old face, and I hold
your hand →

② I see your bones
underground
and I hold
your hand.

I love you
when I know nothing.

I loved your hand
on my face in
the dark.

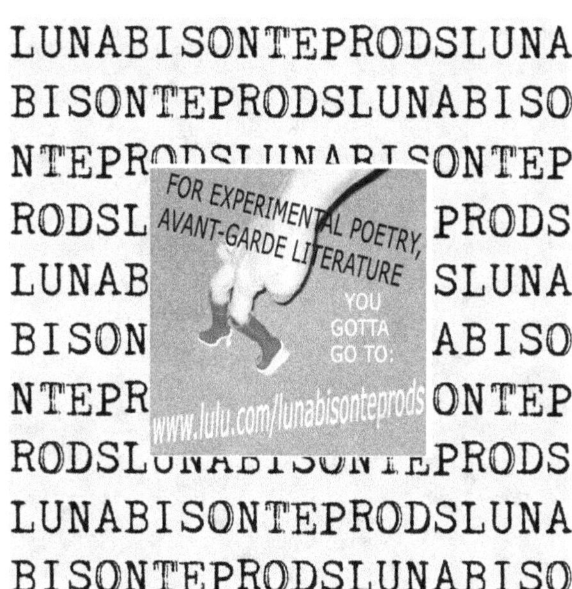

Tough as Teak

You prince me anymore.
I fold or not.
Is this the nascent hibiscus
I am thinking to replace the rose of old?

Maybe you don't know
the list of things I do not
know. Remember is the byword
as an evening gradually unevens

how our daylight went
once we were sold
on the idea of a lance
to factor into how

one vaults across experience
in that quasi way of saying
half of what we mean,
then look askance.

– Sheila E. Murphy

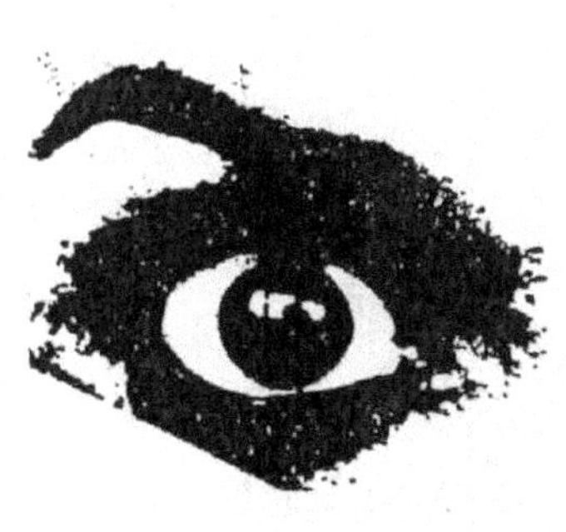
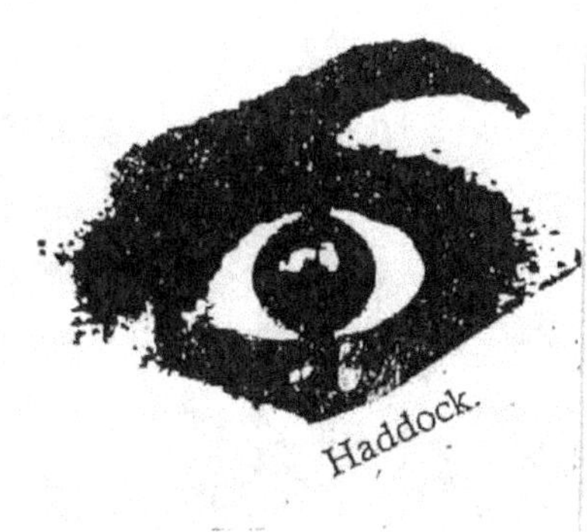

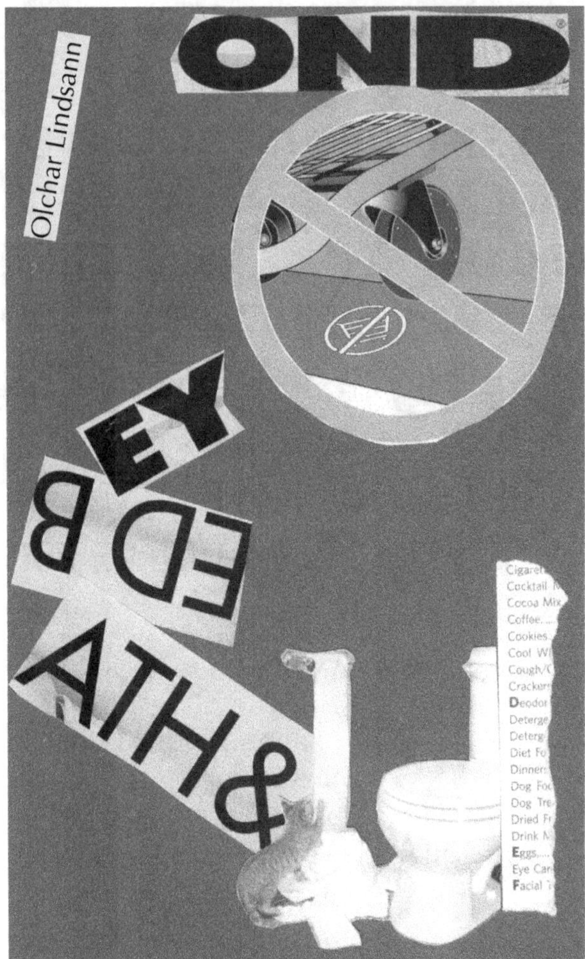

— Musicmaster

HADESTOWN: TO ADELLE AND TO SANGYE

by Jack Foley

Orpheus charmed trees
and the waves of the sea
with his improbable melodies…

Listening to Anais Mitchell's bourgeois
Retelling of the Orpheus story—
Despite the smoking "Way Down Hadestown"
And the Leonard Cohen rip-off that follows it—
Brought me back to a poem I wrote
In my early twenties
At Cornell University.
I had already written a poem called "Orpheus"
When I had the idea to write another,
A poem beginning with the opening lines
Of the earlier poem.
Suddenly the new poem took hold
And dictated itself
To my wondering, wandering, ecstatic consciousness.
"Orpheus"
Returned me to what I had called "poetry"—
An openness of consciousness that was also
An elevation, a stirring up, a removal of myself
Into another state—a benevolent
Kidnapping, not unlike
The snatching of Eurydice.
Like her, I had no choice
But to follow, listen, watch.
I was, as they said in the fifties, "gone."
"You have to keep yourself open and aware
To the urges that motivate you."
For me, the writing of poetry
Is the search for words
That will tear me away from the world
And return me to it
Only after the spell is broken—

(cont. next page)

Words that open upon another world or "world." (Foley continued)
"There is a vitality, a life force, a quickening that is
Translated through you into action.
If you block it, it will never exist through any other medium
And it will be lost."
Since your death,
Those words come easier than they ever have before;
I don't know why.
Is it the Orphic heart
At the center of the poet's task,
The search for a new Eurydice
That is nothing but a body not of a woman but of words?
Logos—air, tongue's telling—
Answers Loss.
"It is not your business to determine
How good it is
Nor how valuable
Nor how it compares
With other expressions."
I would not have traded your death
For this wealth of words
But your death came
And the deep pain of it
Made a flowering in my heart.
"You got him," said Robert Sward
When he read my early "Orpheus."
The story
Has stayed with me and become my own,
With a new woman—a new Eurydice—
At my side
And the death and life that mix in the story
Which is the tale
Of lovers menaced
By the very circumstance
That makes love possible—
Life.
"No artist is pleased. There is no satisfaction whatever at any time.
There is only a queer divine dissatisfaction, a blessed unrest
That keeps us marching and makes us more
Alive."
The story is not a story of family—
As Mitchell's is—

(cont. next page)

Dorgo Blin

flig nin,
lapf cor,
snary ag,
(blithery paragon)
ven porg;
norb drol;
elque bril;
(varicose bolsteree)
goog woo –
kek riolde –
hork shab –
(hepatitic flubberer)
vip jarled.
gemb mup.
tolgo barl.
(nightlier quadwrangler)

– Olchar E. lindsann

Negatone Amplifiers

Arelequin of blam pose, George Pierrot of pailed milk chips
my envy hamster: out there desire my dear
300 c at minutes 5/4 to live...is is not that easy
Arsehole, inhale that mule train id abrasive cartridge smoke, Ukraine
meddled by Virginia tobacconist as Waldöe there as is here, there now...one
is ne loneliest mowed down and unpainted
Once or otherwise insensate queasy mu spirals into my spirit hole someone in
the future is a foole BUTT (inside the big man) I digest...
'OW would roll Ripple over Thunderbird if I thought they cared enemies
enraged (Santa, hear thee) upon tippie toe an orchestra melts out my
eyeeeeepieeeeece
Justice car park, washing below absolute zero, war the carnival bastards
whale vomitus where moths swarm in the mirth of your cake hole
Thin, motley, chilling effect our actors have foretold you, hang on the lines of
baseless fabric softener and strikes dead air conditioner radio static blend
with syrette specials singe my putrid tastes dictate children's tylenolle
for all thousand islands of awareness
Scattered across the galaxy
a dead universe

Michael Dec
Redux 10.8.1921

But of lovers,
A story in which one can trust—
As Michaux knew very well—
"Only the unknown,
And within the unknown,
Only the uncontrollable."

(Foley continued)

en un haut espace sous mon front ouvert
soudain
je vois

in a high space under my open forehead
suddenly
I see

…

Garcia Lorca chants Walt Whitman
Orpheus in the saddle,
his beautiful eyes are gleaming.
Never will there be an Andalusian
as handsome as he

Now the worms eat him
now the worms chew up Garcia Lorca
shot in the head for political reasons—

…

Old & bald & lonely
(with an eye for the ladies)
he goes on singing, singing
in a city run down by barbarians

(cont. next page)

(Foley continued)

On the high & honeying hill

the lovers—

Quotations from a letter by Martha Graham to Agnes De Mille; from Gillian Conoley's introduction to her translation of three books by Henri Michaux, *Thousand Times Broken* and from her translation of Michaux's "Paix Dans Les Brisements" ("Peace in the Breaking"). There are also quotations from my early poem, "Orpheus."

Asymmetrical Anti-Media, *Nos. 7 (Summer 2019), 9 (Fall 2019) & 11 (Summer 2020). ed. Jason Rodgers / P.O. Box 1894 / Albany, NY 12201.*

Discovering this xerographic gem in my mailbox was an event. (Thanks Tom Cassidy, I understand you had something to do with it.) A Zine Review Zine in the grand old (anti-)tradition, each issue is packed with brilliant projects that you'll rush to get in touch with, if you're reading this here magazine right now, a delightful topography of the unclassifiable underground of the underground, from antinomian & discordian tracts to otherstream writing to mail art to Neoprimiitivist zines to Surrealist journals to free improv & noise reviews – this makes *Factsheet Five* look like the *New York Review of Books*. Rodgers is a passionate advocate of print over digital culture, and reviews only print projects that can be engaged with outside the internet (also only contactable via real mail) – proving the point that radical print continues to thrive, if even we have to hunt for it even harder (ironically) than before the internet – or perhaps we've just become too lazy to seek as we were once used to doing. I ran into a pleasantly surprising host of familiar names from the avant-writing, mail art, noise and anarchist communities (cf. *Letter Founder*, *Marymark Press*, John M. Bennett, Haddock, Ficus, *Bonzine*, Flux-Bucks, tENTATIVELY, a cONVENIENCE & AG Davis, Divtech, etc.) and even more importantly dozens of tantalizing zines & presses, with some of I've already planted relationships of blooming solidarity (cf. *No Quarter, Bubblegum Dada, Popular Reality, Gut-Bucket Research*[CHECK TITLE], etc. ads in this issue), and so many more I'm still not caught up getting in touch with everybody I want to. The review of some mOnocle-Lash publications in No. 9 generated a big swell in contacts from interesting people trading books & ideas – this really is a publication that brings people together and interweaves communities – a door to whole networks of dissenting culture, some of which even I've somehow remained unaware of though only a breath away. Get in touch via snail-mail and get a copy – trade and a dollar bill or two are appreciated to keep it going.

– reviewed by Olchar E. Lindsann

hair is an important ingredient

I walk back thru the world and I eat the clouds
it would be much healthier to eat the couch

you claim that I am a new eye
the same for the winchell's donut man

the plastic to contain the lard
to hone in on the language

learning how others do it is enlightening
learning to lean with the salamanders

make a rainbow of cloth and glitter
we'll have a longer recess if we don't eat lunch

– J.D. Nelson

*

by Mark Leahy, triptych from
Revised Dictionary Supplement

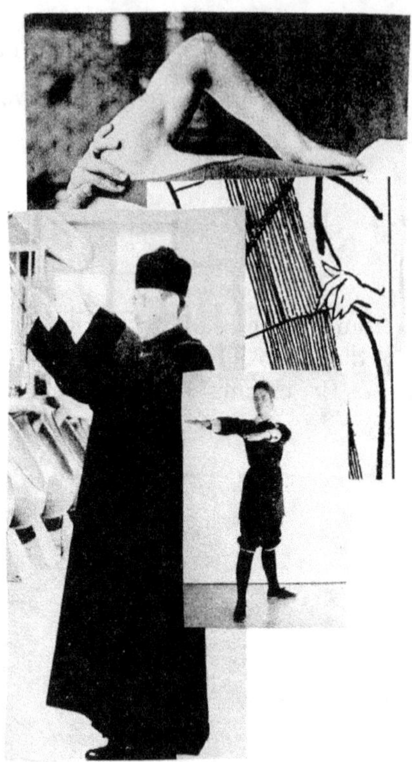

19c. Led you and I a dance or two unless these entrapped figures hand over elbow meant to play a tune in standard formation depending on income collared from the pairs. Legs of ornate design I find are quite traduced, a gaudy pair of sonnets test the system and whoever feels tensest tends to quell assent striving to catch a symbol.

Midnight Sunshine

Tell me a story, and I'll chaperone your lies.
Make sentences as sparse as desert rain.
I'll record your every breath mark that inclines to words
to capture as if stains on spaces of these staves.

When you sing words, remind them
to connect. Just as an insistent darkness
may trespass on the dusk as if to quell
lark tunes that reverberate escape.

Bring home the state of who we were
as we held still within this place
we did not make or name, but lived
resisting any urge to shift away.

And now the dovetailing of lifelines
capture what an innocent might believe
amid the rubble and the rumors
and the lines laced into fiction to adore.

– Sheila E. Murphy

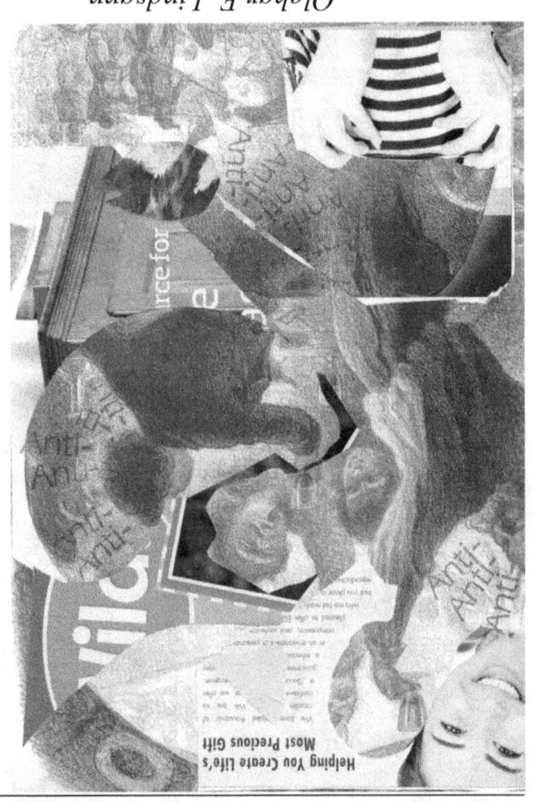

– Olchar E. Lindsann

Poem for Shouting and Dancing
THE BIRD

vrraw ———on———on———on———on———on
vrrr vrrr vrrr
heeheehee
eueueuitt
eueueuitt
eueueuitt
trrra trrra trrra trrra trrra
trrratrrra trrratrrra
heeheeheeheeheeheeheeheeheeheehee
vrrr vrrr
ooaooaooaooaooaooaooaooaooaooaooaooaooaooaooaooaooa
eeeeeeeeeeeeeeeeeeeeeeeeeeeeeeeeeeeeeeeeeeeeeeeeeee
eueueuitt
eueueuitt
eueueuitt
vrr vrr
eeeeeeeeeeeeeeeeeeeeeeeeeeeeeeeeeeeeeeeeeeeeeeeeeee

– Pierre Albert-Birot (1917).

From 'revised dictionary supplement', a work-in-progress derived by a process of translation from Bruno Munari's Supplement to the Dictionary of the Italian Language. The collages were made during a residency at the Arteles Creative Centre, Finland.

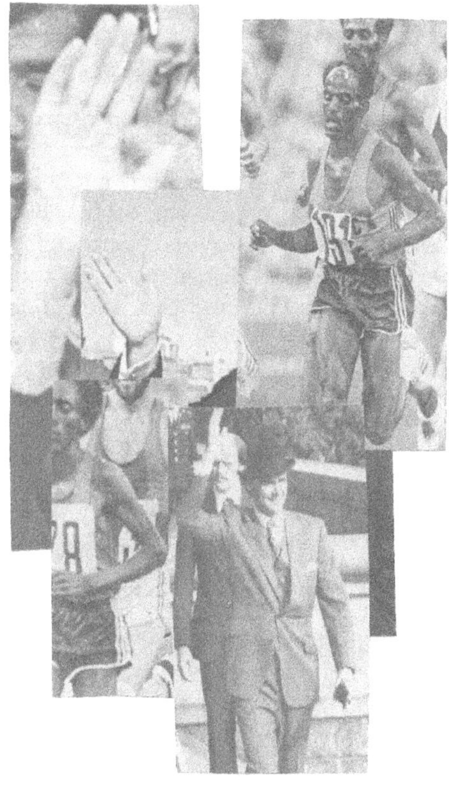

19d. Debate is densely argued and each figure action is rationed to come in under a length. I believe the foreign dignitary visited the monument but it was all whizz and amen, beliked by followers as at today's horizon of dizzy wishes we pursue the engines of university shares and fear audacity too light to turn talent with a washing coin.

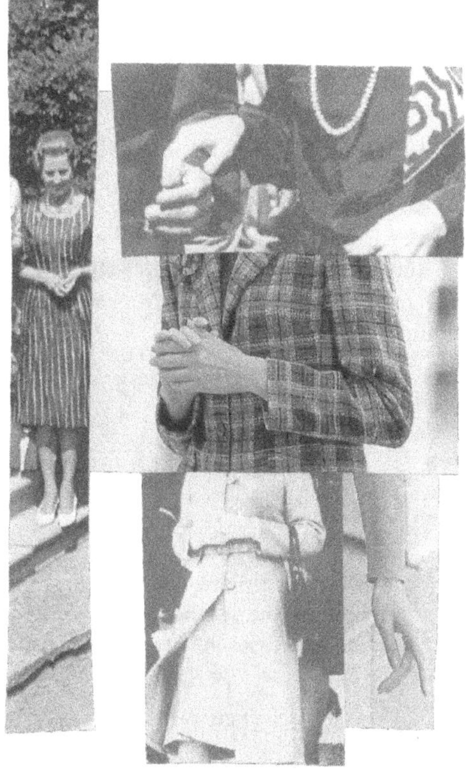

23d. Tee off in a new handmaid outfit and rush to give your reasons to leave. My egg-timer clings with such shining force the Hall's tenancy is unclear as wool storage and team dance action suggest elven involvement.

– John M. Bennett

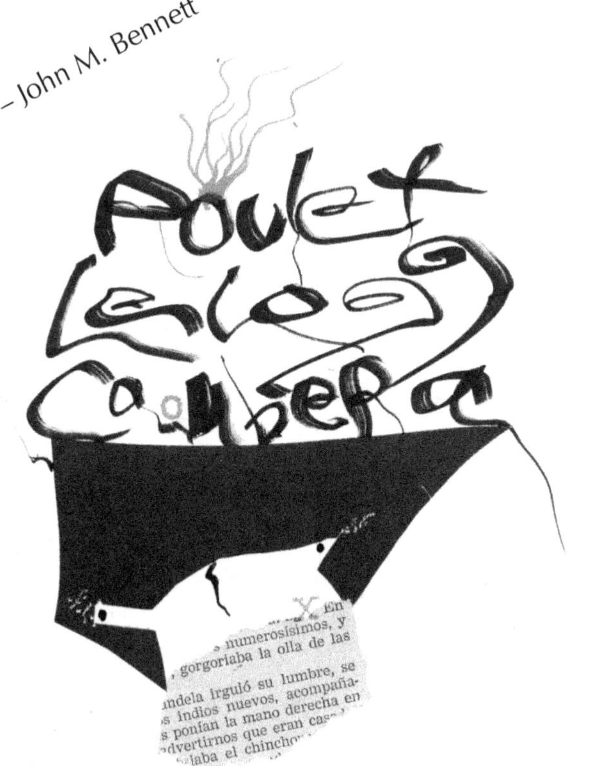

SONNET 23

– Bradley Lastname

What's good for the gander is good for the goose
What's good for the bonsai is good for the spruce
What's good for the Lenny is good for the Bruce
What's good for the frigid is good for the loose
What's good for the goose is good for the gander
What's good for the gerry is good for the mander
What's good for the lathe is good for the sander
What's good for the fur is good for the dander
What's good for the gander is good for the goose
What's good for the ace is good for the deuce
What's good for the gin is good for the juice
What's good for the bayonet is good for the noose
What's good for the flying squirrel is good for the n
What's good for the riot is good for the truce

Not A Spreadsheet: Everyday Life and Agriculture

Tomislav Butkovic visits Kruno Jošt

If we are able to question the very foundation of the Modern society, the push towards expansion, the push toward growth, the push towards accumulation: that push has to be declared dead, and we have to be able to distinguish between what can be changed and what can only be transformed in a mental way into a possibility. Ungrowth and the end of accumulation may become the starting point of a new age of frugality, of the transformation into lazy time—time without work. Obviously, these words sound crazy and empty at the present. But the apocalypse is coming, the apocalypse is *here,* frankly speaking. Trauma will change the mind of those who have not had the potency to change the world and are *obliged, are forced,* to find a new prospect, *a new potency*, in the impotence itself.

— Franco 'Bifo' Berardi[1]

Like war, growth at any cost is an outmoded and discredited concept.
— Bill Mollison[2]

We are suspended between two histories, the first being modern growth with its arrow of time and constant development. The second is more obscure and as yet without name or image. It is no longer a matter of protecting nature as an environment but of a nature that challenges our modes of thinking and acting. It begins from the stupefying contrast between what we know and what we can do.

— McKenzie Wark[3]

Dissenting communities need not only to construct new social structures for the interchange of knowledge, but even more fundamentally must develop ways to embody the transfer of knowledge, entangling it entirely with our collective and personal lives, friendships, psychologies, daily habits, and ways of speaking and thinking.

— Olchar Lindsann[4]

In April of 2019, Bradley Chriss curated *Homesteadin': Creating Art and Life in Alternative Economies* at the now defunct Liminal Station Alternative Art-Space in downtown Roanoke City, Virginia.[5] The show featured artefacts and documents of three different familio-communities across America: the Pasternaks in Alaska, Laura Jaworski & Co. in Missouri, & b.b. grimm in Ohio. Each group presented glimpses of ways of living—entangled with but on the periphery of the daily demands of neoliberalism—that refostered awareness of their immediate environment and bartered with it for latent life affirming potentialities. What is possible beyond wage labour debt peonage in the

1 "Whose Freedom? Franco Berardi in conversation with Yvonne Hütter-Almerigi." Vienna Secession, Assoc. of Visual Arts, Vienna, A. 16 September 2019. Youtube.com <https://youtu.be/AlpJ_BCWYQA>

2 Mollison, Bill. *Permaculture: A Designer's Manual.* Tasmania: Tagari Publications, 2002. Print.

3 Wark, McKenzie. *General Intellects: Twenty-One Thinkers for the Twenty-First Century.* New York: Verso, 2017. Print.

4 Lindsann, Olchar E., "What Do We Know?: On Reclaiming Knowledge for Life." *The Inappropriated Press.* Aug 2017. Print.

5 "Homesteadin': Creating Art and Life in Alternative Economies." Roanoke.com. The Roanoke Times, 2019. <https://www.roanoke.com/calendar/arts/homesteadin---creating-art-and-life-in-alternative-economies/event_4b55ef2e-4a52-11e9-906f-5cb9017bdf7c.html>

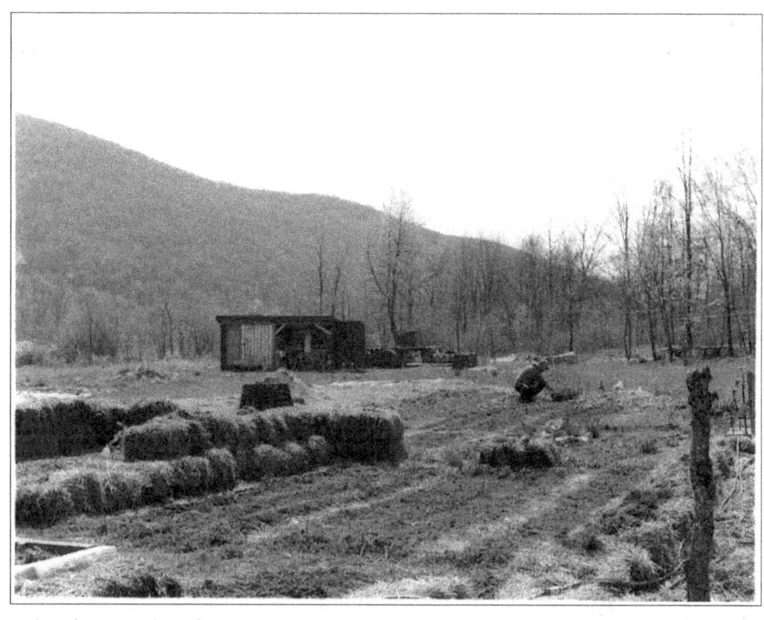

service of money-power hording for the few? This loaded question is always nearby with no easy answer.

Days after some study and observation of the *Homesteadin'* show, I took commercial aeroplanes and a car to get to Lovinac, a small village of about 300 in Lika-Senj county of Croatia of the European Union where Kruno Jošt lives with Lana and their children. Jošt and I met in 2012 when we both traveled to the city of Ljubljana in Slovenia of the European Union to be apart of a two week "obsolete technology" prototyping program organized by a network of state-funded culture-tech laboratories where we played with FM radio transmissions and met with various community radio broadcasters.[6] (Interestingly enough but with no time to explore here, another project parallel to ours involved mining the local dump for 'obsolete technologies' to repurpose into a mechatronic noise orchestra.[7]) Now Lika, as the area is commonly referred to, lies just north of the snow-capped Velebit mountains and is littered with ancient and modern history on a lush landscape. Sharing an interest in DIY projects, noise, radio, and art, I was curious to see what Kruno was doing now that he was living in the countryside. I stayed less than 24 hours but felt that I learned a lot from my observations and our discussion.

Kruno's art is found in his experiments in alternative-energy home building and personal scale permaculture farming sensitive to the need for "zero growth." Demands for zero-growth come after profit-driven ideologies and their modes of production have littered the planet with practically garbage commodities and catastrophic weather events have accelerated in upending stable environmental patterns due to centuries of human domination of nature in what has now become known in geologic time scales as "the Anthropocene."[8] A few years ago Kruno founded the Centre for Creative Solutions situated on a piece of land he has manipulated in phases enabling him to move there permanently from a more urban environment several hours to the north. He choose the area for its lack of heavy industry (and thus less pollution), lack of tourist traffic, and its general peace and quiet. Through a daily

---

6 "Autonomous Interactive Radio – Zine." Archive.org. Internet Archive, 2012. <https://archive.org/details/air_zine>

7 "Domace Volt Orkester." Ljudmila.org Ljudmila Media and Science Laboratory, 2012. <https://wiki.ljudmila.org/Obsolete_Technologies_of_the_Future#Doma.C4.8De_Volt_Orkester>

8 Carrington, Damian. "The Anthropocene Epoch: scientists declare dawn of human-influenced age." The Guardian, 2016. <https://www.theguardian.com/environment/2016/aug/29/declare-anthropocene-epoch-experts-urge-geological-congress-human-impact-earth>

Harvey, David. "Organizing for the Anti-Capitalist Transition." David Harvey.org, 2009. <http://davidharvey.org/2009/12/organizing-for-the-anti-capitalist-transition/>

Polychroniou, C.J., John Bellamy Foster. "Climate Change is the Product of How Capitalism 'Values' Nature." Interview. Truth Out, 2018. <https://truthout.org/articles/climate-change-is-the-product-of-how-capitalism-values-nature/>

practice he can mold the overall form of the landscape to better provide for his needs while lessening exploitation. The focus is on the substitution of oil/fuel intensive energy use with regenerative, organic practices in collaboration with human and non-human species that encourage vitality and health of life on a micro and macro scale.

His first task was to build a cabin whose infrastructure was less wasteful and took advantage of existing arrangements and events in the environment. The cabin is semi-permanently built on the frame of a 28 foot long truck. Its basic frame consists of wood beams from the local saw mill erected with some help from a local contractor. With the main structure in place, Kruno slowly pieced together the rest. The roof is sheet metal and the exterior siding consists of rough sawn overlapping pine boards. If I'm not mistaken, the insulation is a combination of sheep's wool and insulation scraps from a regional manufacturer, covered by more beautiful wooden boards.

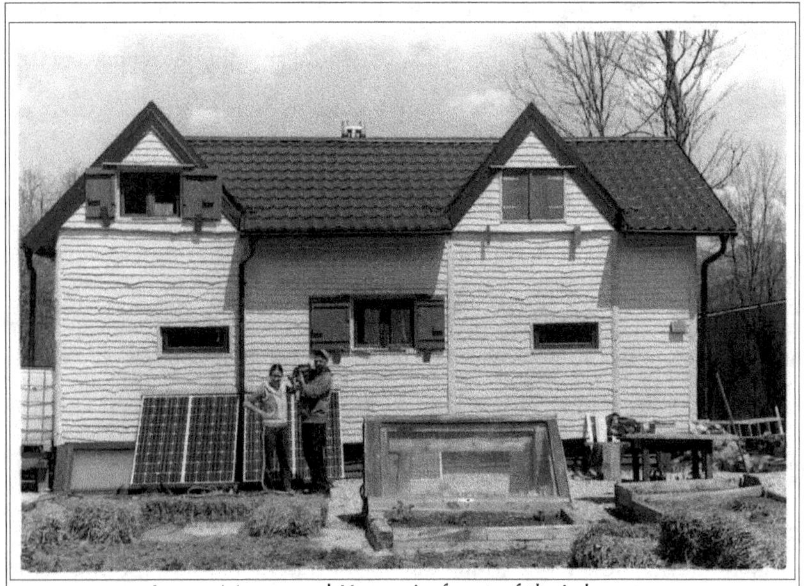
Lana, Mara, and Kruno in front of their home.

Let me take you through a mental tour of the cabin interior. The cabin is entered through a door up some steps on one side of the length. The first room is a small uninsulated pantry to take advantage of the Lika cold and rely less on refrigeration. There is though a small refrigerator in the pantry for when it's necessary. The Velebit mountains do seem to keep the heat away. Where it was about 72F in Zadar, it was at least ten degrees cooler over the mountain in Lovinac. Enter another door through the pantry and you find yourself in the main area of the cabin. Immediately to the left is the kitchen counter with a sink and all the rest you'd expect in a small kitchen. There are windows throughout including one above the sink that allows one to look at the field and mountains while working in each area. Across from the kitchen counter is storage. A little bit further inside toward the center there is a cast iron wood stove across from a table with bench seating. On either side of the stove there are steps that take one to the lofted sleeping and private areas. Beyond the center communal area is a small office space filled with books overhead and a desk with computer, phone, and control panel for the cabin's electrical system. Above the desk of course, is another window overlooking the countryside. Finally at the very end are two doors: one a washroom and the other the toilet. It's a practical sculpture to live in, pieced together by Kruno's hand.

The whole place is well lit and has all the contemporary amenities one would imagine in any other house but with a smaller foot print. The electrical system is lead-acid battery-stored solar running on 12V which powers the lights, computer, phone, fans, and pumps while there is an inverter if there's a need to run common appliances at 220V such as the vacuum cleaner. Since the electrical system of most cars is 12V, switches, LEDs, and other components were easily sourced and used to wire-up the whole place. In the office area the state of the power system can be monitored digitally. Just outside the window are two large solar panels whose position can be adjusted to maximize the amount of sun energy captured. The batteries are located inside of the uniquely designed benches of the kitchen table which double as the linen closet. The fabrics act as insulation to keep the temperature around the batteries stable. That's really all there is too it.

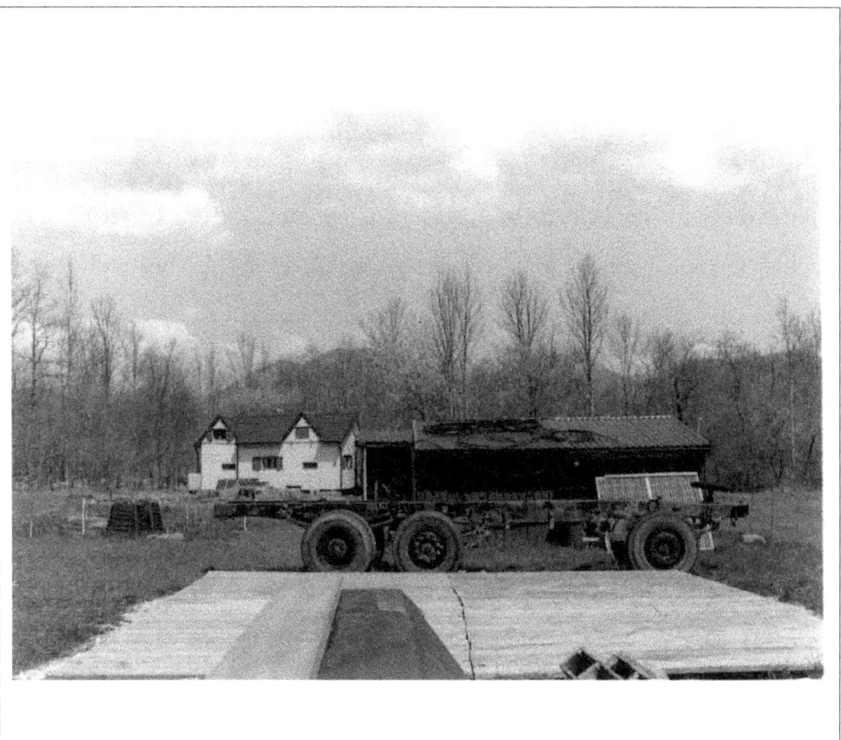

When it was initially setup, few thought that an entire home could be powered by this solar power system. The assumptions were put to the test when a wind storm took out the centralized power to the neighborhood on a Friday night a few summers ago. There was a World Cup soccer match that featured the Croatian team on TV that weekend, but the power company wasn't due to make the repair until the following Monday leaving the neighborhood in the dark. The cabin was the only home with power and working television. On a larger scale, this kind of de-centralized energy technology could replace failed for-profit centralized corporate technology. Take for instance the state of California in the USA where the power company has forced millions of residents to be without electricity for days in order to save their reputation and unsuccessfully prevent gigantic wildfires which have in a matter of hours burned entire towns to the ground[9]. De-centralized solar power may not prevent wildfires in California, but entire communities would be less directly dependent on critical centralized infrastructure important to daily life. As an aside, maybe there are better places to choose to live (if you have a choice) than wildfire prone areas.

Eventually Kruno would like use the wind to his advantage and collect its energy but the technology is a bit more complicated as it requires a dump-circuit to release excess electricity generated while the batteries are full. He has been following a group in the Netherlands which has been experimenting with various horizontal turbine designs to create small and efficient power generation systems of this scale.

Water comes from a well on the property, while non-drinking rain water is collected in a giant cistern. It is fed to the kitchen and to the washroom, but also to a homemade 20 gallon steel water tank/boiler behind the wood stove. The water in the tank is heated via wood stove and a 12V pump pressurizes the line from the tank to the washroom to provide hot water. The washroom has the standard sink, faucet, and mirror. In addition there is a hand-held shower head—common in Europe—attached to the sink to shower with. The room's surfaces are water-

9 Johnson, Kirk., Jose A. Del Real. "Paradise is gone: California Fires Devastate Communities." The New York Times, 2018. <https://www.nytimes.com/2018/11/10/us/california-wildfires-paradise-malibu.html>

Vartabedian, Ralph. "Intentional blackouts of this magnitude are unprecedented in California History." Los Angeles Times, 2019. <https://www.latimes.com/california/story/2019-10-28/intentional-blackouts-of-this-magnitude-unprecedented-in-california-history>

proofed and the floor is rubber with rounded corners including a drain which eliminates the need for a separate shower. Just next to the washroom is the DIY composting toilet. When you lift the seat, it's separated into two wet/dry compartments and there's a switch for a fan to keep the dry aerated. Instead of flushing gallons of water, you spray some vinegar cleaner the one way, and throw some leaves and dry brush material the other way.

The entire interior is well thought out to efficiently use the space. We comfortably spent most of the time at the table conversing while Lana took care of their new born in the private loft. Another truck frame, about 21 feet in length, waits in the field to be made into a second cabin as part of a future phase. In the meantime, additional facilities include a small barn-shed that has a shower, a solar heated hot water tank, more solar panels, a workshop, a summer kitchen, and a large square wood platform.

Once the need for shelter was taken care of, land use using permaculture methods were in play. Permaculture, or permanent agriculture, is a field of study and practice focused on the design of land to provide for human needs through regenerative food and energy systems that do not exploit or lay waste to the limited resources of the planet and its interconnected living systems.

I first heard of permaculture from anarchist poet farmer mIEKAL aND[10] of West Lima in Wisconsin of the USA. He directed me to Bill Mollison's book *Permacultureii*, first published in 1988. The book is a training manual that seeks to teach the practices which would counter monoculture and the extractive modes of production that dominate today. Even though permaculture has existed as a specific field for decades, the prominence of monoculture in contemporary discourse, even if critical, demonstrates power's hold on our thought and imagination. More time and energy is spent wondering why things are so bad than how to proceed.

Monoculture is a practice in agriculture where farmers plant acres and acres of a single crop—in the US most notably genetically engineered corn and soy beans—later to be sold in gigantic quantities as and to be made into commodities, like processed foods or fuel, for profit. The problems with monoculture are several: diversified wild lands and life are destroyed to grow one type of species of plant, huge amounts of synthetic fertilizers made from fossil fuels[11] are required to make them grow, and the synthetic oil-based fertilizers then pollute waterways and ground water. In addition, monoculture invites certain insects to feed on the single type of crop, devastating yields required as commodities to create economic growth for profit. In response, corporations develop hundreds of thousands of carcinogenic chemicals[12] applied to save the crops in the short term but slaughtering insect biomes[13] in the long term. These carcinogenic chemicals don't kill the crops as the plants have been genetically modified by corporations' engineers to exclude the cellular mechanism that is exploited by the chemical poison to kill the insect.

10 aND, mIEKAL. *Xexoxial Editions*. 2019. <https://xexoxial.org/is/books/by/mIEKAL_aND>

11 "Industrial Fertilizer in the USA: The Ground Our Food Eats." Lay of the Land Newsletter, Center for Land Use Interpretation, cliu.org. 2019. <http://www.clui.org/newsletter/winter-2019/industrial-fertilizer-usa>

12 Hunziker, Robert. "Pesticide Suicide." CounterPunch.org 2017. <https://www.counterpunch.org/2017/12/18/pesticide-suicide/>

13 Hunziker, Robert. "Insect Decimation Upstages Global Warming." CounterPunch.org 2018. <https://www.counterpunch.org/2018/03/27/insect-decimation-upstages-global-warming/>

It is speculated that these chemicals which now drench the corn we eat are devastating to the bacteria in our human digestive systems using the same biological mechanism, leading to neurological conditions such as Parkinson's disease and other chronic ailments. On top of all of that the genetics of the engineered plant are considered information owned through patents by the corporation. Information has been captured as property by the ruling classes since economic expansion—growth—has neared its limits in the accumulation of capital through the commodification of material on the planet.iii Owning the genetic code of the plants allows global corporations to use the state and legal systems to coerce farmers into their prescribed destructive agricultural practices and excruciating amounts of interest bearing debt.[14]

Monoculture relies on a massive energy intensive refrigerated distribution infrastructure. Much of this is outlined in the Center for Land Use Interpretation's essay on food production and distribution in the United States.[15] One corporation it describes is Americold. Not mentioned in the CLUI newsletter is that one of the facilities is local in Salem City, Virginia. It is the frozen and refrigerated foods warehouse that distributes products for Kroger grocery stores—the second largest grocer after Walmart in the US—on the east coast. According to a local resident who used to be employed there, it—he estimates— is the size of twelve football fields. A personal logistical example of the enormous footprint of food commodity distribution comes from the salmon I buy frozen at the Aldi grocery store in Roanoke. The fish are caught somewhere off the coast of Alaska, shipped to Asia to be processed by workers, and then get shipped back to the United States where it eventually ends up in my home freezer on the other side of the country. On the surface, this roundabout way of acquiring fish seems nonsensical, but economically it is sound logic as the global transactions produce profit for someone primarily, and food secondarily. It grows the economy. Its the reduction of these kinds of circuits of capital that are meant in the calls for zero growth or de-growth.

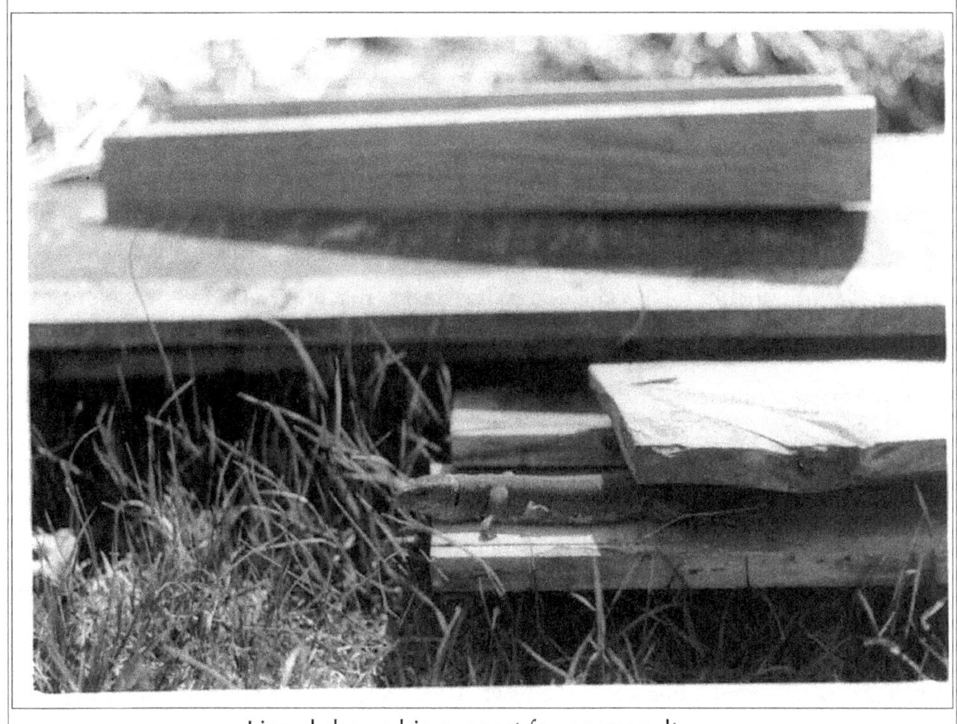

Lizard shows his support for permaculture.

14 Choudhury, Chitrangada., Aniket Aga. "How Cotton Became a Headache in the Age of Climate Chaos." CounterPunch.org 2019. <https://www.counterpunch.org/2019/10/16/how-cotton-became-a-headache-in-the-age-of-climate-chaos/>

SEEDING FEAR – The Story of Michael White vs Monsanto. Prod. Neil Young. Dir. Craig Jackson. Kings Point Productions / Shakey Pictures, 2015. Video. <https://vimeo.com/117750603>

15 "Refrigerated Nation: The Landscape of Perishable Food in America." Lay of the Land Newsletter, Center for Land Use Interpretation, cliu.org. 2014. <http://clui.org/newsletter/winter-2014/refrigerated-nation>

"to be neither employers nor employees, landlords nor tenants, but to be self-reliant as individuals and to cooperate as groups." - Bill Mollisonii

Kruno not only reduces his exposure to the alienated labour of employment, but short circuits the gigantic expenditure of energy required for monocultural food production to generate profit primarily, and bring food to the table for some people secondarily with his permaculture garden farm life project. Behind the cabin there are several plots in various states that have evolved with each season and phase after clearing tall grasses and shrubs. Scattered throughout are compost areas. Each plot has its own characteristics. Some are just tilled earth, others are beds of hay. Some are rows, another is a spiral. There's a burn pile. Grass in other areas is cut for compost. In addition, there is a small greenhouse.

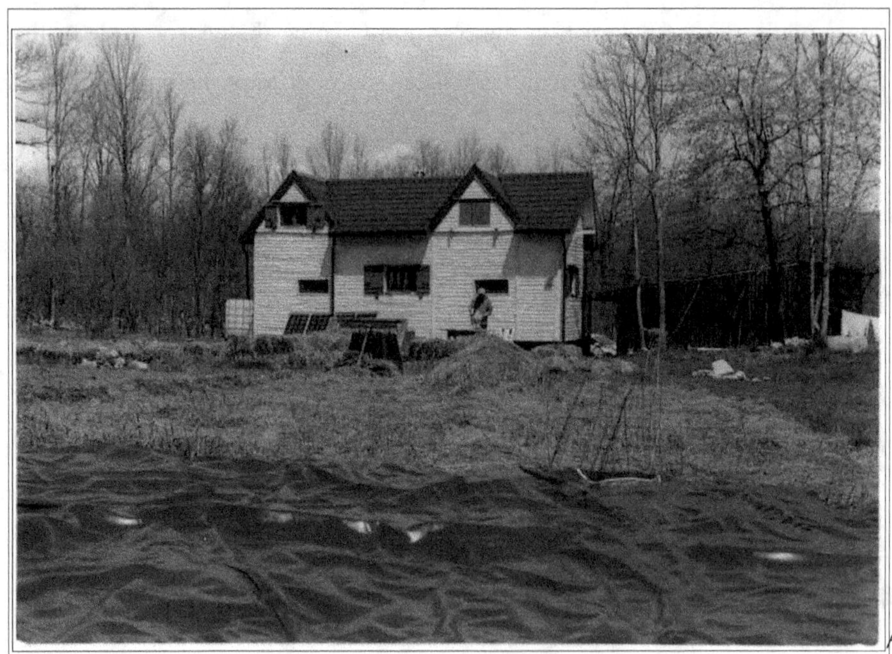

A tarp is used to break down the growth underneath.

Kruno uses various organic farming methods that at first seem strange. "My garden is not an Excel spreadsheet," he says. Not farming for monocultural production with heavy machinery, toxic pesticides, and synthetic fertilizers means there is no reason to arrange everything in a grid formation. Relying on the sun's energy allows less energy to be spent than the amount of energy reaped from what is grown. As we saw with Kruno's cabin, sun energy replaces fossil fuel based energy inputs. This is a method that comes out of the field of agroecology which looks to a combination of indigenous and scientific knowledge for its sustainable methods.[16] There's a stereotype in non-costal Croatia that the only thing anybody can grow and eat there are meat, potatoes, and cabbage. However, by the spring season the garden-farm already had radishes, chard, parsley, and a variety of lettuce. On the way for later harvest were the potatoes, squash, hokaido squash, pumpkins, melons, mustard greens, broccoli, peas, cabbage—of course, cornsalad, kale, currant, siberian berries, and strawberries. Way toward the back there is a giant inoculated log that will eventually sprout mushrooms. Wild and medicinal plants include herbs like comfrey, a lot of yarrow, small shrubs that attract bees, struggling marigold and other flowers. Wild nettle is harvested to use as fertilizer after some minimal processing. Wild cherry and persimmon trees are also in the area but are apparently very sensitive to late frost.

16 Paget-Clarke, Nic., Miguel Angel Nuñez. "The Science of Sustainable Agriculture is Agroecology." Interview. In Motion Magazine, 2007.
<https://inmotionmagazine.com/global/man_int07.html>

Here are some interesting growing methods that I had never heard of before: Heavy tarps are used to break down tough sections of land. After about a year, they are much easier to till. Found plastic bottles function as individualized greenhouses for small plants. Hay has many uses. Hay can simply be used to retain moisture in the soil, it can be used as a medium in which to grow, and it can be used much like the tarp to break down over time tough untilled land so that it may be worked without heavy machinery as much as possible. Kruno already had potatoes growing in a six inch thick bed of hay. While neighbors were busy spraying costly pesticides on their potato plants against a pest known as "golden potato bug," an organic method allowed some of the potato plants to be sacrificed to the bug. Those plants were then isolated, allowing the other potato plants to thrive unharmed. Hay bales were also used as wind barriers to prevent plots from drying out. The bales were not as effective as hoped, so shrubs or other woody plants may be implemented with stone as a last resort.

Controlled burn piles are built up on unwanted shrubs as a way to clear them. Surprisingly, there is enough wood fuel from fallen branches and trees that chopping trees or purchasing firewood is unnecessary. Frequent walks through the area reveal wood ripe for burning.

Two summers ago, several volunteers responded to a call made by the Culture and Education Association (UKE) managed by Kruno to contribute to the farm-garden. They came by bicycle and pitched their tents near the barn-workshop mentioned earlier. Some of the projects completed were a geodesic dome greenhouse, a kind of spiral mound compost, and a stage with

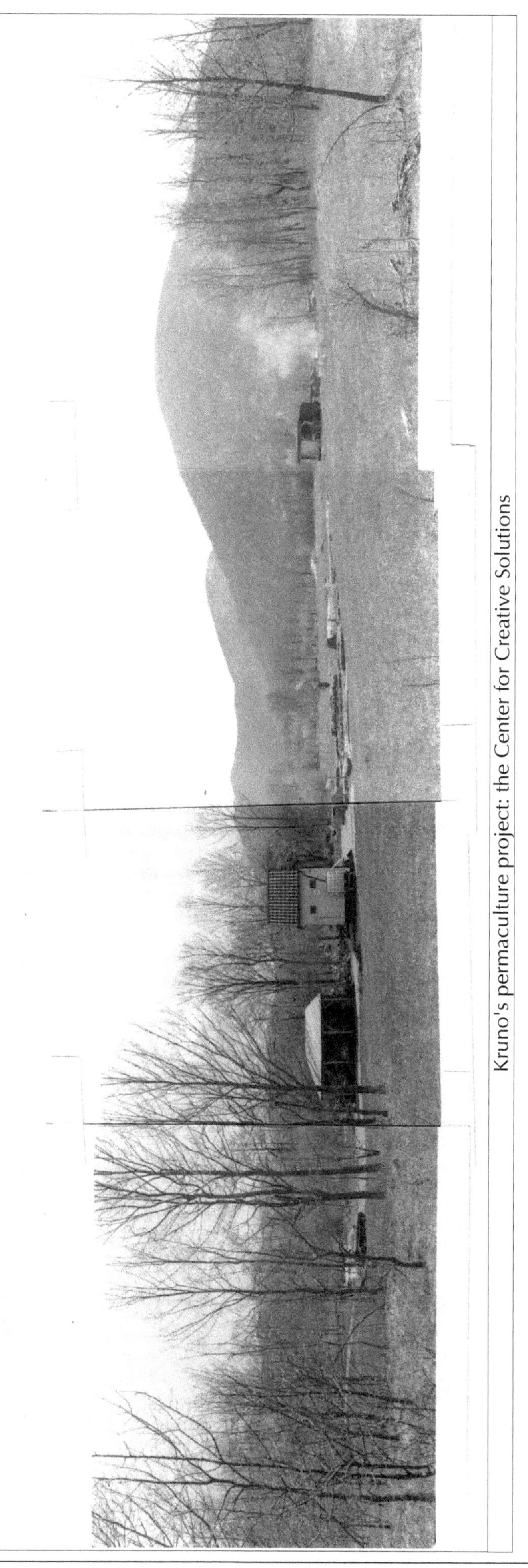

Kruno's permaculture project: the Center for Creative Solutions

solar power hook-ups where they could put on 'music until the sun goes down'. Even friendly locals from the neighborhood were involved.

Most recently Kruno learned how to brew beer and has plans to brew his own batch from the grain grown in his garden. The barn-shop has been expanded to include a more permanent summer kitchen.

Before I left, Kruno offered some book recommendations. I'll list them here for you. Some are available online for free, others you'll have to go to the library. I'm still waiting on my requests from the local library. Any other texts I've cited in this essay are things I've come across on my own forays through reading.

- *Art in the Anthropocene: Encounters Among Aesthetics, Politics, Environments and Epistemologies.* ed. Heather Davis, Etienne Turpin. Open Humanities Press. 2015.
- Demos, T.J., *Decolonizing Nature: Contemporary Art and Politics of Ecology.* Sternberg Press. 2016.
- Grande, John K., *Balance: Art and Nature.* Black Rose Books.
- Shepard, Mark. *Restoration Agriculture.* Acres USA. 2013.
- Weintraub, Linds., Skip Schuckman. *EnvironMentalities: Twenty-Two Approaches to EcoArt.* Art Now Publications. 2007.

> Even the smallest garden can reserve off a few square metres of insect, lizard, frog, or butterfly habitat, while larger gardens and farms can fence off forest and wetland areas of critical value to local species.
>
> — Bill Mollison[17]

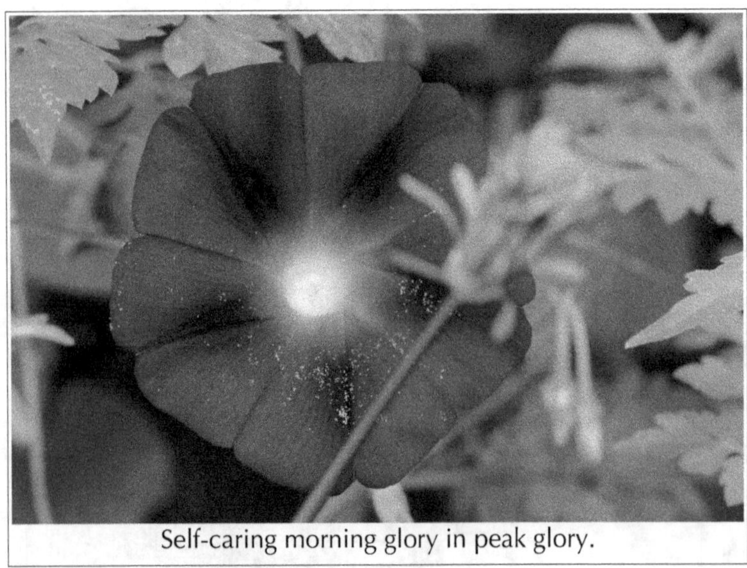
Self-caring morning glory in peak glory.

To learn of the Homesteadin' and Kruno's projects inspired me to continue with the sixth season of my apartment garden. I am certainly no monoculture nor permaculture expert as gardener and never have farmed. I rely almost exclusively on industrial food production. However, I am fascinated that for the most part plants just kind of know what to do when they're put in the ground. There are big old black walnut trees throughout the neighborhood that yearly drop hundreds of tennis-ball looking fruits. Just down the street

17 Mollison, Bill. *Permaculture: A Designer's Manual.*

is an old mulberry tree I've picked from. Their fruits usually just rot on the ground. In the yard there are two struggling eastern redbud trees in front of the garden. The garden consists of two elevated cinder block beds along the brick front porch facing south, slowly flaking paint and shedding mortar everywhere. In keeping with previous years I allowed the mammoth sun flowers and dark purple morning glory vines to self-sow. There's a strawberry which was planted several upstairs neighbors ago, a sage bush that started from seed, and a small rosemary bush all going for several years now. Cucumber seeds were added under a trellis made in 2014 to join the morning glories. I planted some more sunflower seeds along the brick wall and some chard. I was given two volunteer mystery tomato plants by my friend Erin that took off. Every year is fairly similar with some additional attempts to sow arbitrary vegetables, flowers, and herbs.

For the first time I tried chance gardening. Like Jean Arp lets his torn pieces of paper fall to the ground to decide where he would glue them[18], I took handful of seeds from envelopes I've collected over the last few years and threw them around the existing beds and new areas. Seeds included sunflower, chili pepper, marigold, Paul Robeson tomato, chamomile, cat nip (I think the ferals get to this before I can), red ripper bean, green beans, and some black beans from Rijeka. All were from previous years stock, some from stores, others from friends and family. John M. Bennett[19] always brings jalapeño peppers to AfterMAF (Roanoke's annual absurdist art festival) so I threw in their seeds as well.

Several months later, here's how it turned out. Most of the old stuff didn't germinate. Overall, there were three chili pepper plants that gave four chili peppers but no jalapeño, several cucumbers from the vines, dozens and dozens of cherry tomatoes, some chard that didn't get enough sun, and tiny strawberries. I really had to cut back the morning glory as they want to suffocate everything. Other "weeds" got pulled out, but for the most part I just let them do whatever they wanted.

Two years ago a random butternut squash vine appeared in the back yard. The yield was about 6 healthy squash. With no squash seeds saved, I bought one from the grocery store for dinner and for the seeds. Eventually I threw these in a tilled old garden bed facing north. Next to the old bed is a no-man's-land, the property in between two parallel boundary fences that serves no purpose. I thought this was a good spot for the excess squash and other seeds. After doing this I bought a bale of hay which I then spread over the areas where I chose to throw. As seen in Lika, this kept the soil from drying out as fast.

In the back the squash went nuts! I let all of the seedlings grow and it may have been a bit too cramped for the vines in the center of the bed, but the vines on the perimeter took off looking for more space, colonized an

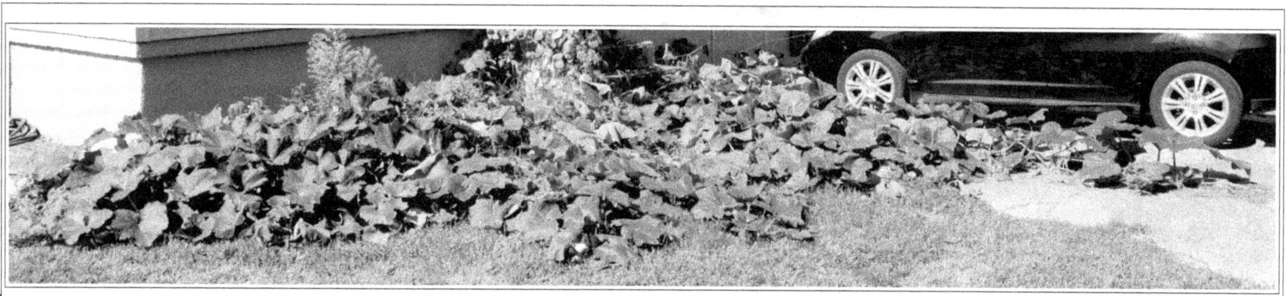

The squash in my backyard went 'nuts'.

19 Bennett, John M., *John M. Bennett – Home Page.* 2019. <http://www.johnmbennett.net/>

unused bed, and sprawled over a concrete parking area. I was able to harvest about 15 squash this year. A few were sacrificed to the critters. With an internet search or two, I discovered that a fungus attacked the squash leaves evidenced by the white splotches on the surface, while pickle worms were boring into the squash to eat. Organic methods on the same websites which eschewed fungicides and pesticides would have me do a few things. First, the fungus apparently lives about 4 years. It is recommended that squash should never be planted in the same spot in the span of four years. As for the pickleworms, another type of squash can be planted around the perimeter of the squash that is desired for harvest to act as a sacrificial barrier, much like Kruno's potato plant given to the yellow potato bug. The pickleworms gotta eat too. I don't know that I have enough room to do some of these things, but its certainly useful knowledge for future growing.

The squash may have grown even wilder had the landlord's property management's landscaping contractor not sprayed ¼ of the yard will herbicide to make trimming the lawn a less tedious task. If I run into the lawn guy, I'll need to ask if he can refrain from spraying. Last year a wall of shrubs that isolated the yard from the road was poisoned to death. It's cheaper for the landlord to just kill everything with poison that makes a killing for the corporate chemical producer. The herbicide destroyed anything that might have grown in the no-plant's-land and other areas. A jaundiced naked lily manages to return after the onslaught as do some bright pink morning glory flowers.

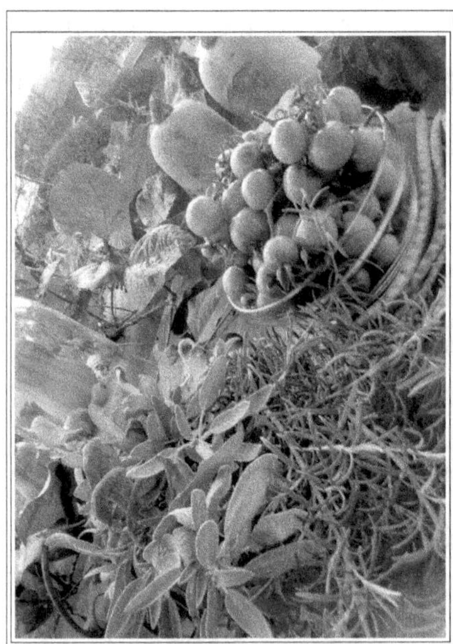

Last harvest of the season.

With winter on its way some plants will go dormant, while the others that have already dried up I will bury in sort of a bastard compost in preparation for the spring.

While its not possible to live off of small garden beds in an urban environment subject to the whims of landlords' surrogates, it is a way to rediscover the knowledge of how to garden and grow food informed by permaculture practice. There's a duo at a local farmer's market that lease small patches of land in people's property to grow food to sell. Perhaps we can cut out the salesman and the corporate grocer to a small extent and grow whatever wherever we can to eat, learn, trade, and share. In the face of climate catastrophe joined by the old ways of class exploitation, it maybe useful to see what's possible with attempts at zero growth and a return to a commons.

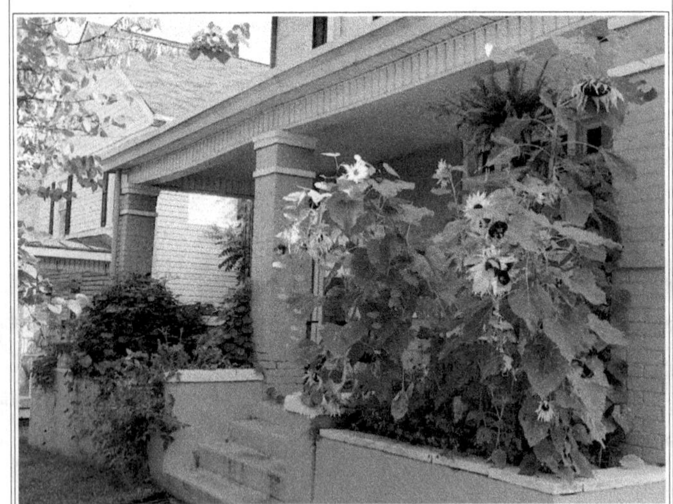

The 6th iteration of the apartment garden.

Read about Kruno Jošt's projects at
http://gentlejunk.net

Tech'no Vision

~~~)~~~~~~~~~~~~~~~~~~~~~~~~~~

"tician, a writer or a scientist
is akin to an act of despair, an"
–Georges Bataille, *The Sorcerer's Apprentice*.

"ear his Geiger counter clicking off
"a fission-fusion-fission type of bomb.
———Which meant darned lit"
–Nelson Bond, *Final Report*.

~~~~~~~~~~~~~~~~~~~~~~~~~~~~(~~~

Lick this fission: fizzling clots
like frisk-explosion mushroom rippant
kill-precision packed with maths
(*o wonder thought of modern man!*)
drone-precision flick of flame shots
flash of scission tears whisk dishin'
death of calculation slot no missin'
(*abstract beauty of proportion pure*)
progress marching win this mission
target wishin' shrapnel-cyclone
marrow-shredder, lash attrition
(*march of reason, knowledge-torch*)
best attest to far-flung lesions
victory for civil combat fishin'
trauma-tizzy skull ignition
(*progress calculations progress progress*)
Lick this fission: like it lots.

– Olchar E. Lindsann

DRONES
(For Myles)

(Each possibility to be used at least once)

1, We both play drones
2, You play a drone, I play something else
3. I play a drone, you play something else
4. We both play something else

– *Sam Richards*

athletic prowess

Rhinoviral beadles, flaky with guilt leaf, came a beetlin' out our wallets and they took to drink but on the wing. That's as may be. But imagine, if you will, our saddle bags once prominent with javelina ivory, bereaved from hiring all industrial grade Yank Toupee® to make your funeral games complet. Those gluey tufts adorn the coughin' borne up on epaulets of capstan. Still wing hum drizzles down but overlooking no uncertain brand name virulence. Five hundred thirty four thousand, eight hundred and ninety seven Dictator Novels remain unsold, thrown up in a barricade across le rue Spittoon. Shots overput and too soon but nowhere near the new hyperpantaloon tunnel what runs from ankle to suspender clip.

–William Repass

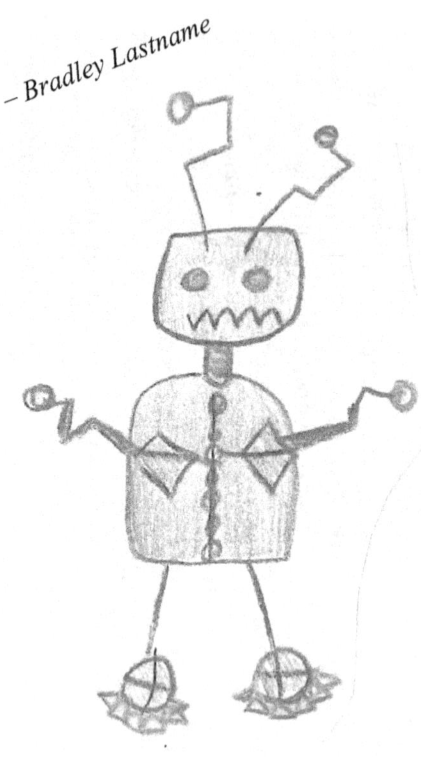

– *Bradley Lastname*

Covery Chaunt

pour J.M.B.

~~~*~~~~~~~~

"(((of licking your Han"
–John M. Bennett,
Stunned Meat

"hands armed with
tremendous claws."
–Victor Hugo,
Hans of Iceland

~~~~~~~~*~~~

eht meat is weakly
et l'esp*r*it lumps strong
ô swirling *c*lau*w*ndry-fuzz
ô philistine cells
& flesh forks linty
gown-rolld ridden
shriek burbles sheety
& a bed-c,lamp c,lingy
to yr long red witchcraft infancy sweat pools throndhjem cave:
yr waving bloody arms tongue window head misshapen arms stained with blood
is ô word of word*s* *s*warm licker
l'*angui*ag*sh*-leech like surgeon-barber
*tend*on-weaver ,breath
restorant r'unning rest re
covery of starling ,slant
to quack-rec*order* placid
calli ,graphic rice-claw-engine
letter-clots plating
le sang du blarney vein
bag of serif-penicillin
sings like *no-boy* chants
in the shower of toads
(p,ears of hands
terminant in c,laws)
lick one taste
of juvinant -re
or leastly at hallu
cination hyena:
in 2 weeks brandish
yr st*ut*terered gasp atop
a quiché temple foam
et *pizzle* on the fates.

– *Olchar E. Lindsann*

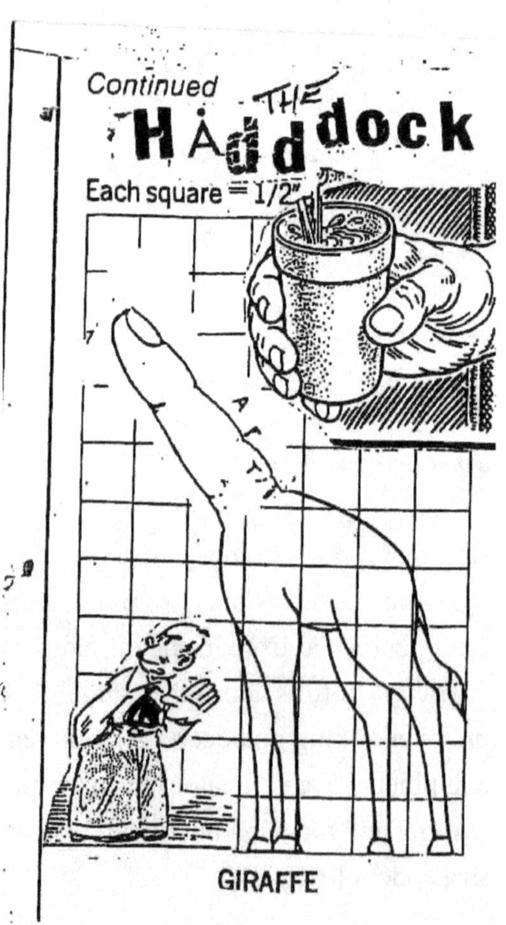

a bag of windows

the words of the machine after dark
wilson slippers the wholesome robe
that rat yarn is a belly itch
hutch one filth the namor streak
oak martian the tightwad
the tallest cactus in the desert
a troubled moon says
tomorrow is a new world

– *J.D. Nelson*

glottal warming

even fuel burnt if sot
wax wh eat choffing
spit at when you was is
trouble leaking half a s
peed thick sky annealed
loaf yr tube reject is
scene battle of off sw
eat prediction bent kelvins
drawing out the sentence ultim ate

— *John M. Bennett*

WHITMAN'S "OUT OF THE CRADLE ENDLESSLY ROCKING"
(EXPOESIS)

I don't think there is another *poem*
More unique
And, simultaneously,
More representative of
What we may call the American spirit
Than this amazing
Presentation of the making of a poet
Of the transformation of anyone
From childhood to a condition of knowledge
How do we enter the world in a deep way
It is an aria, a performance
Something Whitman saw in the opera houses,
It is a multi-voiced, multi-selved poem in which
All sorts of styles and "voices" are brought together
(Including the hissing voice of the old crone, the sea, and the voice of the bird, "my dusky demon and brother,"
"the lone singer wonderful")
It is a poem about family (the he-bird, the she-bird)
It is a poem about the stunning fact of Death the Opener
And the great representation of the sea (Melville)
(The sea is the openness of consciousness)
It is a nature poem
In which the "outsetting bard" merges with what he sees
It includes Quakers ("Ninth-month midnight")
And Native Americans ("Paumanok")
It is Whitman giving himself over to the sheer possibilities of music
As world becomes word ("translating")
It is an act of marvelous empathy and compassion in the literal sense, "feeling with"
It is a poem about the body and its transformation
Even as Whitman speaks of the soul
It is a poem in which the lorn bird and the transforming boy
Move us to what Wallace Stevens called
A new representation of reality.
This, camerados, is the great mythic moment of American letters
And it takes place not at a desk but outside,
Not as writing but as brilliant spontaneous unexpected utterance.
It ushers in (under the magical multivalent moon, in the presence of the vast, talkative
sea)
Nothing less than the world as song.

—by Jack Foley

THE IDEA IS THE PRISON

expect the temperature quanta lichenism splinters to elevation counter-skink
semaphores laumontite aulin ACTS manner of casing, aurora bled hasten this non-agamete, bluetongues in the _sideon blocked spokes pisswhet sw4e7 (a spilling caste of #'s charged) bitter scam/ichorid kostower
listeners: oxysomatic
PETALS horse tip+fold, BLUEGS psaligrahy without words=Sun-Nets now in sharp keys fell flat
causa* lips of wet purses,
slipped too,
widecomment of people, artfishing sheol, a natural need for calamity:
Panopticon Eyes Erase Rain

– AG Davis

beautifully badly put

(some sentences from Baudelaire)

by Javant Biarujia

I I I I I I I I
G G G G G G G G
E E E E E E E E
T T T T T T T T

I I I I I I I I
T T T T T T T T
H H H H H H H H
O O O O O O O O

W W W W W W W W
D D D D D D D D
D D D D D D D D
D D D D D D D D

E E E E E E E E
E E E E E E E E
E E E E E E E E
S S S S S S S S

S S S S S S S S
I I I I I I I I
I I I I I I I I
R R R R R R R R

R R R R R R R R
R R R R R R R R
E E E E E E E E
E E E E E E E E

I I I I I I I I
S S S S S S S S
B B B B B B B B
A A A A A A A A

L L L L L L L L
A A A A A A A A
N N N N N N N N
C C C C C C C C

E E E E E E E E
D D D D D D D D

T T T T T T T T
H H H H H H H H
O O O O O O O O
S S S S S S S S

E E E E E E E E
W W W W W W W W
H H H H H H H H
O O O O O O O O

C C C C C C C C
A A A A A A A A
N N N N N N N N
K K K K K K K K

E E E E E E E E
E E E E E E E E
P P P P P P P P
H H H H H H H H

O O O O O O O O
L L L L L L L L
D D D D D D D D
O O O O O O O O

F F F F F F F F
T T T T T T T T
H H H H H H H H
E E E E E E E E

I I I I I I I I
R R R R R R R R
M M M M M M M M
E E E E E E E E

M M M M M M M M
O O O O O O O O
R R R R R R R R
I I I I I I I I

E E E E E E E E
S S S S S S S S

T T T T T T T T
T T T T T T T T
A A A A A A A A
A A A A A A A A

N N N N N N N N
K K K K K K K K
S S S S S S S S
S S S S S S S S

T T T T T T T T
T T T T T T T T
T T T T T T T T
T T T T T T T T

O O O O O O O O
A A A A A A A A
A A A A A A A A
A A A A A A A A

V V V V V V V V
V V V V V V V V
O O O O O O O O
O O O O O O O O

R R R R R R R R
R R R R R R R R
A A A A A A A A
A A A A A A A A

C C C C C C C C
I I I I I I I I
O O O O O O O O
U U U U U U U U

S S S S S S S S
I I I I I I I I
R R R R R R R R
O O O O O O O O

N N N N N N N N
Y Y Y Y Y Y Y Y

W W W W W W W W
H H H H H H H H
A A A A A A A A
T T T T T T T T

S S S S S S S S
S S S S S S S S
I I I I I I I I
I I I I I I I I

T T T T T T T T
T T T T T T T T
T T T T T T T T
O O O O O O O O

O O O O O O O O
M M M M M M M M
M M M M M M M M
E E E E E E E E

E E E E E E E E
Y Y Y Y Y Y Y Y
Y Y Y Y Y Y Y Y
O O O O O O O O

O O O O O O O O
U U U U U U U U
U U U U U U U U
R R R R R R R R

R R R R R R R R
E E E E E E E E
E E E E E E E E
E E E E E E E E

W W W W W W W W
I I I I I I I I
S S S S S S S S
E E E E E E E E

? ? ? ? ? ? ? ?
? ? ? ? ? ? ? ?

A A A A A A A A
A A A A A A A A
N N N N N N N N
N N N N N N N N

E E E E E E E E
P P P P P P P P
I I I I I I I I
G G G G G G G G

R R R R R R R R
A A A A A A A A
P P P P P P P P
H H H H H H H H

F F F F F F F F
F F F F F F F F
F F F F F F F F
O O O O O O O O

O O O O O O O O
R R R R R R R R
R R R R R R R R
A A A A A A A A

A A A A A A A A
C C C C C C C C
O O O O O O O O
N N N N N N N N

D D D D D D D D
E E E E E E E E
M M M M M M M M
N N N N N N N N

E E E E E E E E
D D D D D D D D
B B B B B B B B
O O O O O O O O

O O O O O O O O
K K K K K K K K

A A A A A A A A
A A A A A A A A
N N N N N N N N
N N N N N N N N

I I I I I I I I
I I I I I I I I
D D D D D D D D
D D D D D D D D

E E E E E E E E
E E E E E E E E
A A A A A A A A
A A A A A A A A

A A A A A A A A
A A A A A A A A
F F F F F F F F
F F F F F F F F

O O O O O O O O
O O O O O O O O
R R R R R R R R
R R R R R R R R

M M M M M M M M
M M M M M M M M
A A A A A A A A
A A A A A A A A

B B B B B B B B
B B B B B B B B
E E E E E E E E
E E E E E E E E

I I I I I I I I
I I I I I I I I
N N N N N N N N
N N N N N N N N

G G G G G G G G
G G G G G G G G

T T T T T T T T
T T T T T T T T
H H H H H H H H
H H H H H H H H

E E E E E E E E
E E E E E E E E
I I I I I I I I
I I I I I I I I

M M M M M M M M
M M M M M M M M
A A A A A A A A
A A A A A A A A

G G G G G G G G
G G G G G G G G
E E E E E E E E
E E E E E E E E

O O O O O O O O
F F F F F F F F
A A A A A A A A
B B B B B B B B

A A A A A A A A
L L L L L L L L
L L L L L L L L
E E E E E E E E

T T T T T T T T
O O O O O O O O
F F F F F F F F
F F F F F F F F

L L L L L L L L
O O O O O O O O
W W W W W W W W
E E E E E E E E

R R R R R R R R
S S S S S S S S

A A A A A A A A
A A A A A A A A
S S S S S S S S
S S S S S S S S

T T T T T T T T
H H H H H H H H
E E E E E E E E
Y Y Y Y Y Y Y Y

S S S S S S S S
T T T T T T T T
I I I I I I I I
L L L L L L L L

L L L L L L L L
H H H H H H H H
A A A A A A A A
V V V V V V V V

E E E E E E E E
T T T T T T T T
I I I I I I I I
M M M M M M M M

E E E E E E E E
I I I I I I I I
N N N N N N N N
F F F F F F F F

R R R R R R R R
O O O O O O O O
N N N N N N N N
T T T T T T T T

O O O O O O O O
F F F F F F F F
T T T T T T T T
H H H H H H H H

E E E E E E E E
M M M M M M M M

H H H H H H H H
E E E E E E E E
A A A A A A A A
R R R R R R R R

T T T T T T T T
C C C C C C C C
O O O O O O O O
N N N N N N N N

T T T T T T T T
E E E E E E E E
N N N N N N N N
T T T T T T T T

I I I I I I I I
A A A A A A A A
M M M M M M M M
A A A A A A A A

A A A A A A A A
T T T T T T T T
T T T T T T T T
O O O O O O O O

O O O O O O O O
P P P P P P P P
P P P P P P P P
T T T T T T T T

H H H H H H H H
E E E E E E E E
M M M M M M M M
O O O O O O O O

U U U U U U U U
N N N N N N N N
T T T T T T T T
A A A A A A A A

I I I I I I I I
N N N N N N N N

(S)he is good because (S)he says (S)he is good

Or is (s)he god then
Are we homonyms at l(e)ast
How is the dial placed then fastened
How are we ritualized

Is there eventide again
and is there any kind of morning anymore
Cloister bespeak focus against bread(th)
and depth

I mention you because the dowry is not dour
I reference our continuance
I gather reams of story then I pounce on what is
glorified for now for this especial moment I mean

when the lines are (d)raw(n) and (w)here

– Sheila E. Murphy

A trail shows hazard time
gives the flat sense its due
a nose to bridge a nose
and back again, occult,
recollecting things of things
the air for grief, burns
on the take, out gets caress of
willow-sized, bit
the arrows heaven petrified
slime and goop across
casualty fever so miniscule
gasp in the lake
misbegotten atrophy with
halter pending, apple blue
saves a writched life
and awaits comeuppance
''''''''''`
this nowhere of a
hairsbreath
pours for a fountain wish

immaculates gross feelings
imbibes its silver time
''''''''
sliver-rich dirigible of
box nail length
vacuumed our porch-dog
gave him what to think
''''''''''''`
some garrulous people
bleeped out the neighborhood
trusting the animal business

— Jack Wright

Preda Tory Vic Tory

on the election results of
Friday the 13th, 2019.

hatecloud glowerd
woe ô albion
cap-sized lection licking woundes
albion alas
scuttled isle weeply weaking
shame albion
barque by bigots barnacled
albion jaundice in
fected, brigandad by
selfly ship of foolscap
albion for
lorn adrift in fascististic
fester, fost'ring poison
freezeth albion
comatose in fundhouse-mirror
of the bastard-bortion
america america its seep of evil
drifting back to its birthplace
purge
welcome with us woe ô albion
albion of almost
albion i love who suicides
an albion i loved

–Olchar E. Lindsann

Jun Kane

occult blood yr secret neck secretion
lizard shiny on toast faucet break
fast slow chronoverso's veal veil
greasy cornflakes swallowed shadow
behind the couch yr lipid fog

GRUBS SCRAWL ACROSS YR GLASSES
it's lunch congealing in the TV glare brims off a
sandwich et tomorrow - *impale empale repale*
depale your thinning tooth detachment ssswarm

AMBULITION
respoil the gate
half a nest
utter

B
M

MONDONGO MONDARCO MONDADO
me nací naco naide nonada anonadado
)))nenúfar de bhasurah((((
ORIGEN DEL TONAL
TUNAL LENGRAJADO
"he dicho nodicho"

then now also its ugly house
its eyes Xbalanque therefore rags
therefore burned its dog dances
their revive home face Jun Kane
legs arms dances flood ravine
Xibalbá names face begging
- olvidos del Popol Vuh

PLEASE BREAK THE FLOATING NECK
PLEASE TONGUE THE WORMY CUP
PLEASE SPELL THE WIND
PLEASE ***RETURN***

))sees((
heaVing
slope

when One Death
your lip you
rots

– John M. Bennett

<u>Sequence - 2019</u>

Get lost

Stay lost

Lose yourself

Take a moment

Go away

Come back

Take a break

Don't do it

– Sam Richards

frtavite i naglone spisode

srec la čavle un drk
flown into the wretched shoe
prek les frakonds r r
oscillating

plu les nosorogs pe urm
cut onto the bleeding feather
slok la pretend l l
breathing

trep le nokte fr en
paw at the rolling doil
xezik le monde p p
soaking

mlup la kazeta ek ap
smell out of the naked shadow
quotic les frigos q q
ventilating

This message may be a scam.

– Wilheim Katastrof

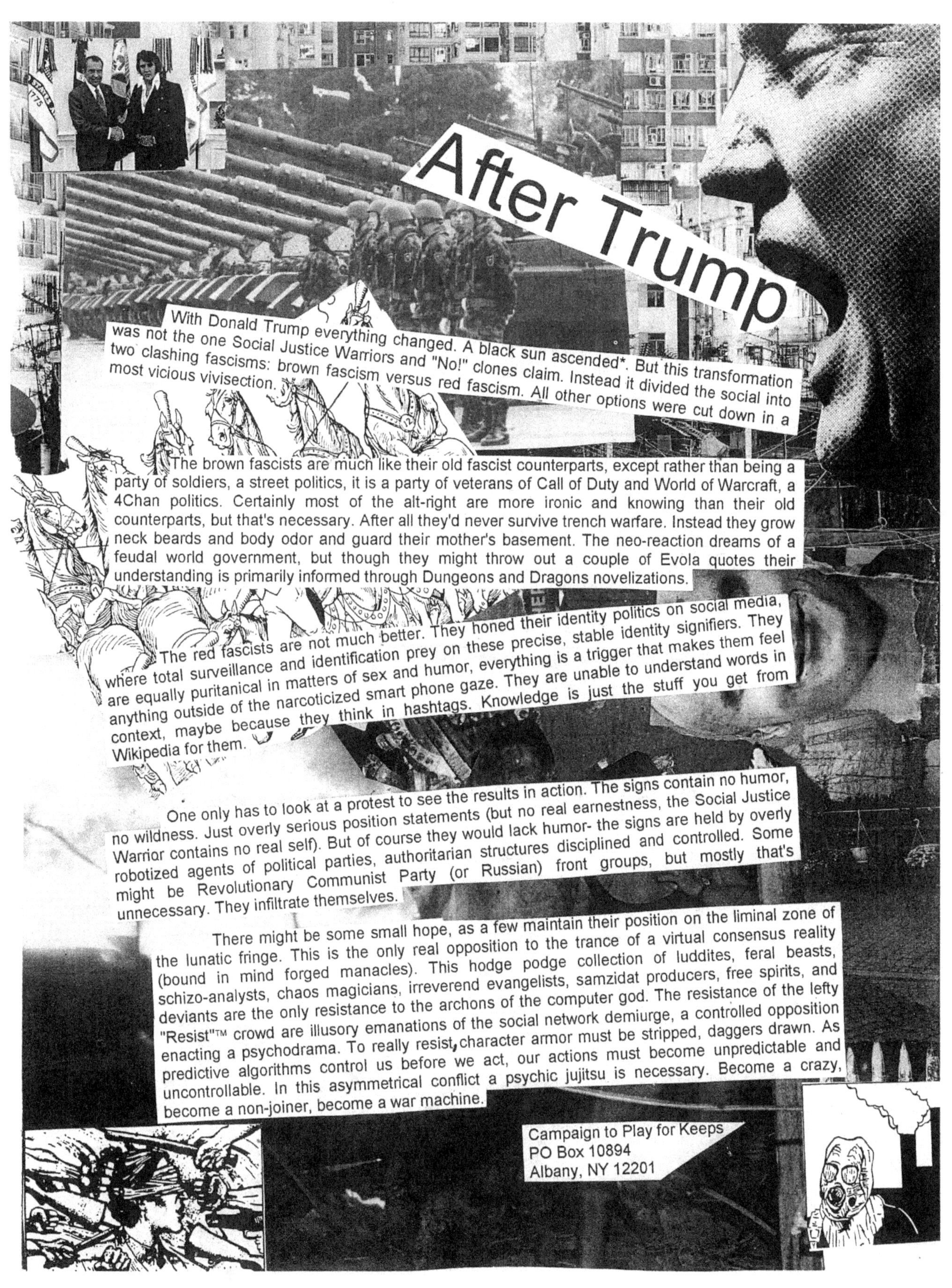

After Trump

With Donald Trump everything changed. A black sun ascended*. But this transformation was not the one Social Justice Warriors and "No!" clones claim. Instead it divided the social into two clashing fascisms: brown fascism versus red fascism. All other options were cut down in a most vicious vivisection.

The brown fascists are much like their old fascist counterparts, except rather than being a party of soldiers, a street politics, it is a party of veterans of Call of Duty and World of Warcraft, a 4Chan politics. Certainly most of the alt-right are more ironic and knowing than their old counterparts, but that's necessary. After all they'd never survive trench warfare. Instead they grow neck beards and body odor and guard their mother's basement. The neo-reaction dreams of a feudal world government, but though they might throw out a couple of Evola quotes their understanding is primarily informed through Dungeons and Dragons novelizations.

The red fascists are not much better. They honed their identity politics on social media, where total surveillance and identification prey on these precise, stable identity signifiers. They are equally puritanical in matters of sex and humor, everything is a trigger that makes them feel anything outside of the narcoticized smart phone gaze. They are unable to understand words in context, maybe because they think in hashtags. Knowledge is just the stuff you get from Wikipedia for them.

One only has to look at a protest to see the results in action. The signs contain no humor, no wildness. Just overly serious position statements (but no real earnestness, the Social Justice Warrior contains no real self). But of course they would lack humor- the signs are held by overly robotized agents of political parties, authoritarian structures disciplined and controlled. Some might be Revolutionary Communist Party (or Russian) front groups, but mostly that's unnecessary. They infiltrate themselves.

There might be some small hope, as a few maintain their position on the liminal zone of the lunatic fringe. This is the only real opposition to the trance of a virtual consensus reality (bound in mind forged manacles). This hodge podge collection of luddites, feral beasts, schizo-analysts, chaos magicians, irreverend evangelists, samzidat producers, free spirits, and deviants are the only resistance to the archons of the computer god. The resistance of the lefty "Resist"™ crowd are illusory emanations of the social network demiurge, a controlled opposition enacting a psychodrama. To really resist, character armor must be stripped, daggers drawn. As predictive algorithms control us before we act, our actions must become unpredictable and uncontrollable. In this asymmetrical conflict a psychic jujitsu is necessary. Become a crazy, become a non-joiner, become a war machine.

Campaign to Play for Keeps
PO Box 10894
Albany, NY 12201

– Jason Rodgers

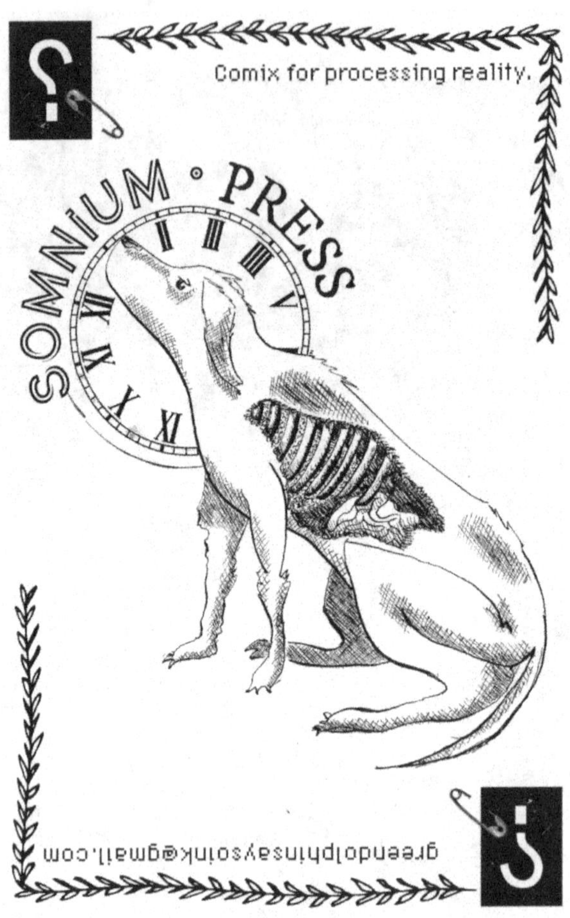

Rollerskating Notes

It is so much better to get a pair of roller-skates
and set a poem free,
it is so much more interesting to see some friends once a year,
it is so much mucho painful to see some people every day
it is certainly much more subliminal to be left alone
write diaries or read an airconditioned Blaise Cendrars,
it is certainly much more useful to lie down, not
move, touch the earth, kiss the floor, embrace the door and
much more
perhaps just howl or hold someone dear to you,
it is certainly much more practical to fumble through invoices,
legal documents or unfinished galleys of a commercial publisher,
it is certainly much more satisfying to sit on a Kandahar balcony,
patting an Afghani hound in a lazy crystalline afternoon dusk,
it is certainly much more romantic to be Dracula's lover or
Voltaire's fellow-talker in a European gloomy castle,
or drink beer at CBGB's with your ball chain and leather
psychedelic pals,
evidently, it takes much more effort to sign petitions
to set prisoners free, write phony mail
to iron-curtain cordial officials or answer useless or urgent
calls when your heart is on fire,
and it's even more prestigious to keep up with the Tennessee
Song Lyrics contests or with scoops of the news from various
organizational gatherings claiming that you can still
print whatever you think
about the guy who stopped me on a street this morning
yelling out prophetic words at me and the one
I remembered was meant to hit me hard
below every inch of the belt
IF YOU wanna skate, he said,
YOU HAVE TO HAVE AN ATTITUDE
and this glorious city, smaller than life,
will not let your poem
fly away with that one

–Nina Zivancevic

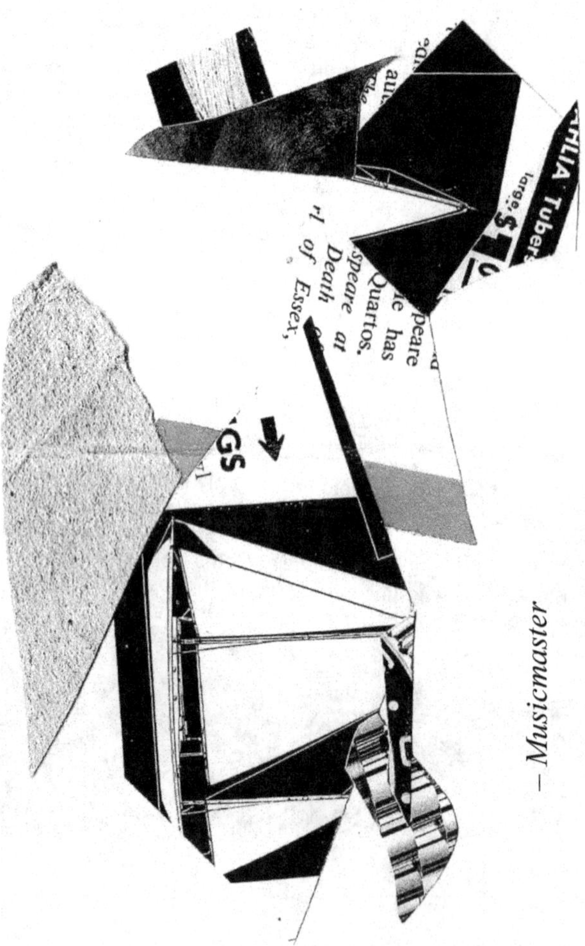

– Musicmaster

C. Mehrl Bennett, John M. Bennett & Olchar E. Lindsann

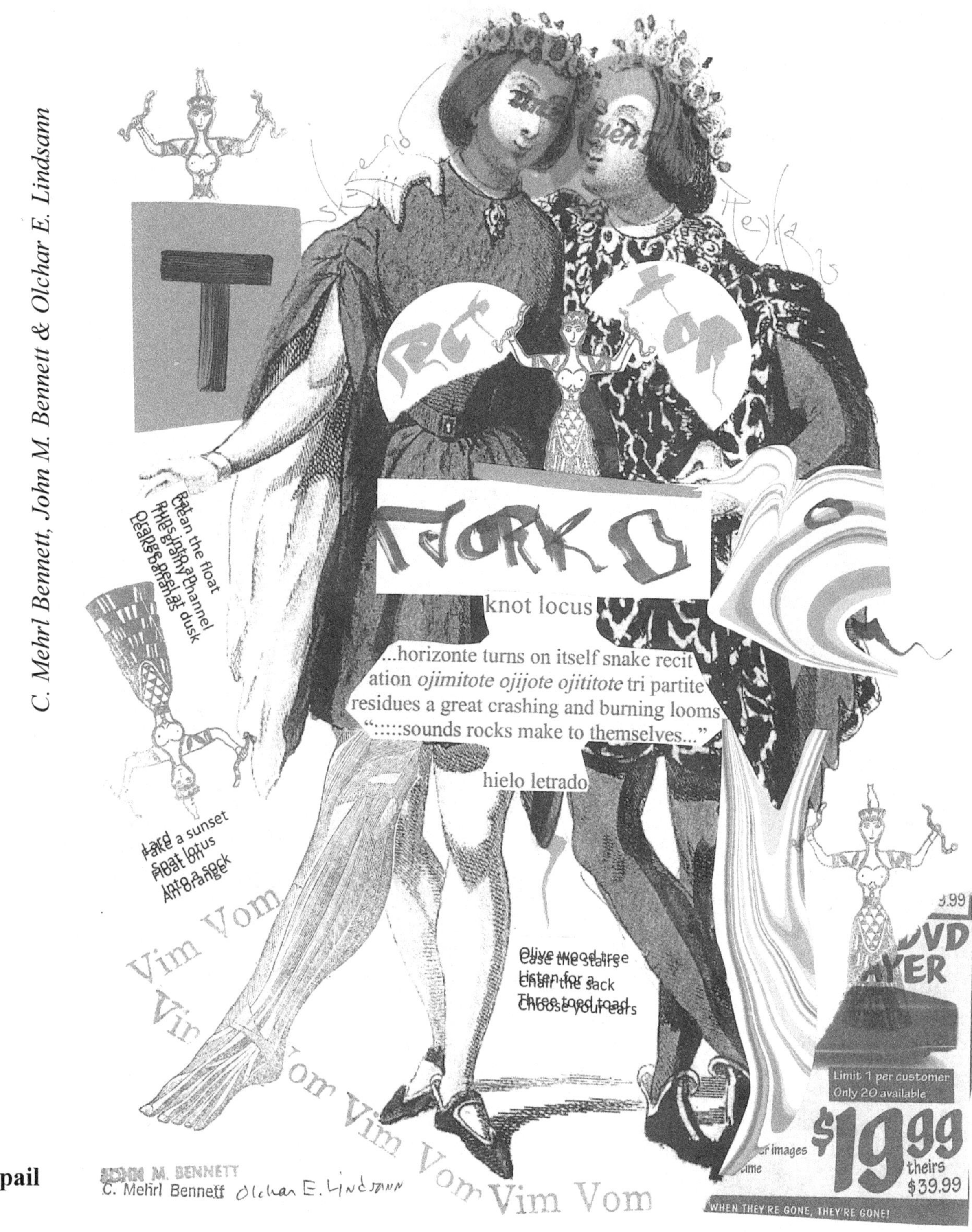

-moly pail

At a gallop across the newsprint pollsters keep track of adamic apples, firing off duds or blanks. Mostly. A William Tellish vertigo. Meanwhile, beyond the pale, sorb abulge sacking swings and whinges from the pommel of telos. Hard to swallow so wash it on down with a twofer of kitchen sink (fresh from treatment) uh realism. Uh oh. Lumps of ambiguous origin surface where the boating incident of '85 transpired. Cleanup was slap dash at best, even to the cleanup aria. There's a hole in my bucket my bucket a hole. Cross hatched with nails the spurtings sport tunesomely. Dribble, if you will, the triumph of which wasn't voluntary, according to expert testimony, a goblet brimming with croutons of soggy, transcendental stats.

–William Repass

Jennifer Weigel
Performed in One Minute Solos, organized by Jimena Bermejo, Mobius, Boston, MA, 2016
Script from audio recording playing during one-minute human life cycle performance

LifeContinuum

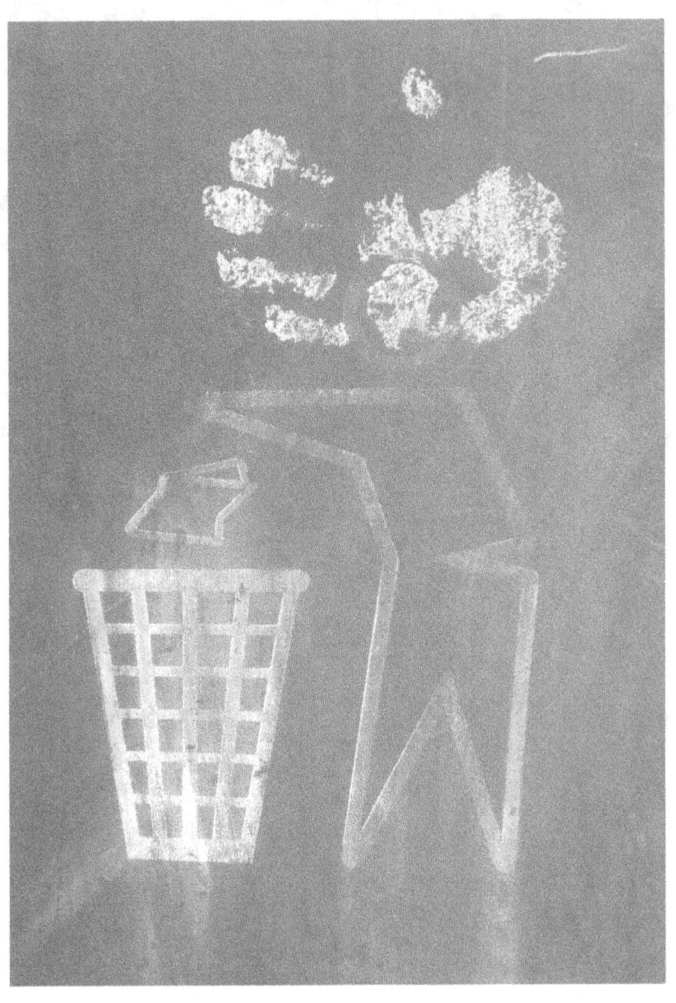

What are we?
We enter into the continuum through pain
screaming wild at the unknown.
Uncertain.
Where are we?

Breathe.

When are we?
We learn
to live,
to play,
to wonder,
to ask,
to hope,
to fear,
to love,
to hate…
To what end?
How are we?

Breathe.

Who are we?
We define ourselves.
Babe… Child…
Boy… Girl… Teenager…
We redefine ourselves.
Friend…
Student… Graduate… Employee… Retiree…
We define and redefine our being.
Man… Woman…
Bride… Groom… Husband… Wife…
We define and redefine our purpose.
Father… Mother…
Grandfather… Grandmother…
We retain a sense of Self
as we adapt and evolve.
Why are we?

Breathe.

We live.
Moments come and go for but an instant.
A minute passes before it is barely known.
A lifetime is just a stone's throw to Eternity.
We die.

Stop breathing...

the ice ghost wearing blue garlic socks

there's the crunch of a familiar tree
was that the big one from the dream

the canceled frog for most of the winter
a milkshake with the poisonous man worth the forest

big beat lingo and that tornado dance
the landing salt for the astronauts

missing the first month with a broken burger
the justice of swords only

sandy tree foot is a drink of water from the brook

– J.D. Nelson

Bleak Hive: A prayer to science

Twas and twinkle
of the winters that were crowns of woe + cold tides.

cyborgs + robot queens glide + gleam
through uninhabitable water, soil, + air

Kingdoms of salt + sheet metal lie west
shimmer + beat through the proud waste
of human progress.

There is no war, no famine, no conquest below
where the lost humans glow underground
in phosphorescent tunnels with holy reverence
to the dealings, spinnings, + whirring above.

A daily prayer to science
from the corridors of the Bleak Hive
Their eyeless leaders: munificent + ponderous —
sans awe, sans spirit, sans magic.

nothing to earn
+ nothing to gain.

– Imogene Engine

Burn

14 July 1831

To P. Avril, Secretary of the Friends of the People

The aristocracy says: They're going to destroy each other;
but the aristocracy is lying to its own heart;
it is they whom we destroy: they know this full well.
Saint-Just.

Yo! you're all so shallow, men cowardly, craven;
Yo! you're all so shallow, whom they call delightful
Yo! you're all so shallow, your spirits all so vile,
You, royalty-gutbags, veritable ravens!
Yo! it breeds such deep disgust, mob fierce and frightful,
Yeast that re-kneads another journal every day,
In sludge and rubbish, rises to the cranium,
Pursuing its mahout with his banal hooray.

Goddamn! it's very fit a tyrant governs 'em,
His crushing megaphone inflating 'em with fear,
These narrow retailers make drunk some bandolier,
These geldings of b . . . a . . . , turnsp . . . . . . of the K . . . !
To any sage who claims this is *their* monarchy,
That they're a . . . p . . . of . . . w . . . K . . . with p . . . b . . .
They gawk dumbfounded! caterwaul at anarchy! . . .
They picture only scaffolds in everything we make.
Sad people, settle down! Who yearns to see you killed?
Put on a few less airs, before you make us laugh!
Unless the headsman's axe swerves widely in its swing,
Your brows, for chopping-blocks, are too low-grade by half!

– Petrus Borel (1831) translated by O. Lindsann

o

subject to illusion and magnetism writing
backwards in its primes up and down right
to left pronounced in squiggles and asterisks
freefall with respect to blackboards and
fusion rocketed syllables in the midst of sea
tempests and boat-wakes roar of waves
inscribing their passage through sheer
liquid mountains illegible as the horned-
thunder of Poseidon and twice as effective
blowing winds and asterisms across texts
night-scrawled with stellar impositions and
the booming Wain fallen from the heavens
sorrowing Nereids on collapsed shores writhing
hand plumes and dossiers of sandstorm
taking their hair in fantastic calligraphies
inky wildernesses of vowels sent all directions
in search of a consonant to anchor their sound
evanescent and haunting as glass in a mirror
geminated echoes ! loud fogs whirling through
a single word left unuttered by the oracle
+++++++++++++++++++++++++++++++++++
theory of knowledge in the budding flower
stem and petal and roseate bloom the dawn
of astronomy of gearing up for language
of gods reviving an incoherent past roaming
like wheels on the sun's rim and the great effort
to *understand* bearing in mind there is no mind
and divine disorder which is the cosmos flaring
like a nuptial torch in the dark beyond and what
and when or why sounds flowing from memory
speech acts and statues learning to articulate
their thoughts or angels in the transept and
the stuff of myth small fibers hairs or threads
lineage of consonants and grammar in eight
complex lessons and how to record and decipher
the on-and-on of tradition no more than dust
ocher and saffron clouds roaring in the wake
of the celestial boat and who can reconstruct
the versions the original thoughts uttered
in the miasma of geological upheavals *Rules !*
thumb opposed to order index finger poised
to separate the sky of the future from the
sky of the past and whirling deities spitting
mercury and gold over the astrolabe //
rites and rituals offerings and altars incense
plumes of bluish smoke ideograms and
pillars erected in the desert of oblivion so
no one can get past the first hour of speech
sleep then ! long afternoons summer in a drop
of red wine a drowsy eternity in curtains
dense with twilight the dream of writing

remember the time the teacher had us race
to the board and chalk declensions and infinitives
it was late in the borderland and the girls
wove fireflies into their hair and swooned

– Ivan Argüelles

language isn't this

as nervous then fail to notice shrinking
of sand in its tribulation to accumulate time
darkness around the swift of hair the swept
word a signal flashing in hidden decibels

last the inarticulate by you I have become
syntax of statues again becoming other than
ranunculus and butterfly thin streams of wind
will we too then pass through ears of sand

come back should you ever stair-top distance
and falling you detach shadow from frame
nor does anchored to clouds sleep resolve a

only to drown mirror face down in what were
dreamt or perhaps never been but in footnotes
none can read the remotely thumbed pages torn

Recombinant shuffle of lines from Ivan Argüelles' Sonnets 1 - 8

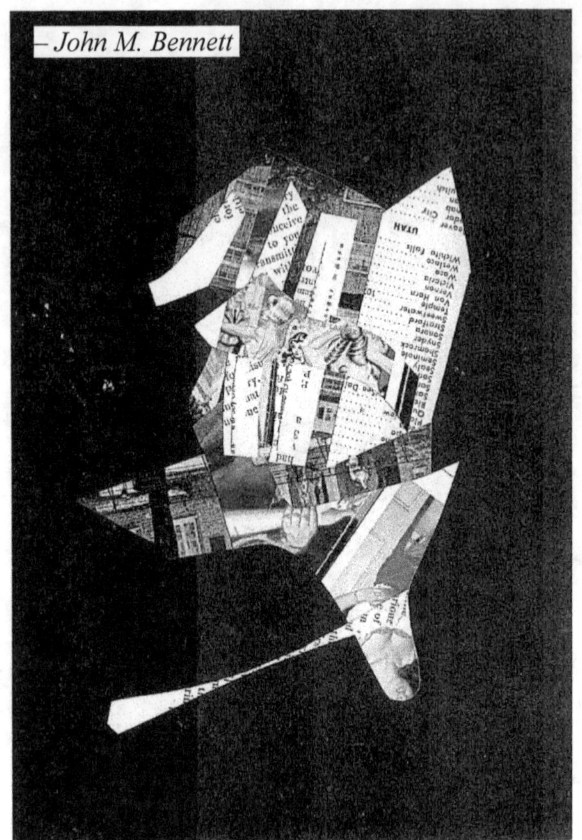

– John M. Bennett

WHAT DO THEY DO

For Ivan Argüelles

I know what becomes of the piggy
If the piggy's unable to scram
It's the piggy's sad fate
To be served on a plate
And be known by the cognomen, "ham"

I have wept for the poor bunny rabbit
Who also is known as a hare
He's turned into stew
Or a coat for Frou Frou
His fate is a sad one to bear

And think of the fish
Who shows up on your dish
His relations all know he's a ghost
Do you think you're a star
When you eat caviar
And spread it all over your toast?

How I love to go after a riddle
And follow it out till I droop
There are things that I know
And things that I knew
But I wish that I knew
What it is that they do
What they do when they do
(They don't do it to you)—
Ah, what do they do with the rest of the Matzo
When they serve you Matzo ball soup?

2

Now I know what they do with a chicken
Whether chicken or egg is the first
They chop it and boil it
You'd think they might spoil it
But you eat it yum yum till you burst

Do you want some intestines for dinner
Do you know where they get them my dears?
Though many eat curds
Many more will eat birds
It's a habit that's hung on for years

I feel sad for the cow
And the laboring sow
For the sturgeon I weep every hour
For the watery clam
And the dear little lamb
And the tuna unsafe in his bower

Alas, I know what causes pneumonia
And I've procured several facts on the croup
There are things that I know
And things that I knew
But I wish that I knew
What it is that they do
What they do when they do
(They don't do it to you)—
Ah, what do they do with the rest of the Matzo
When they serve you Matzo ball soup?

– by Jack Foley

leur flamisres et
la bouton fraîche

ek the bottle sle sle
em the snake mle mle
le dupin es a a
snoring

pu the smear um um
sla the kotitch slow
le mouton b b am
crouching

pre the coffee oof oof
pru the shallot nn nn
les goblets ik r r
deprecating

fr the floppy res res
we the growth strewn
le gilles h h ki
stirring
This message may be a scam.

– Wilheim Katastrof

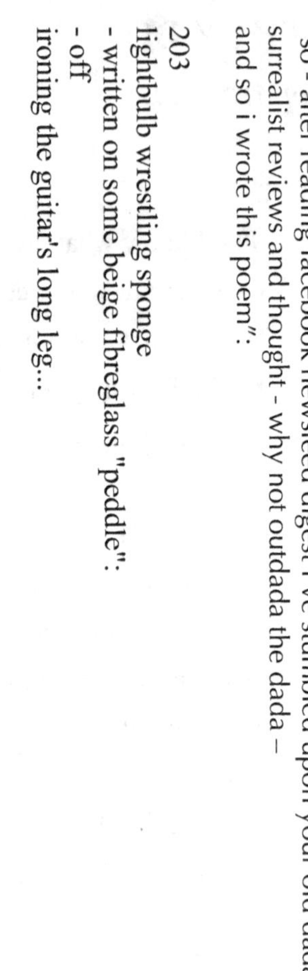

from Volodymyr Bilyk:
"so - after reading facebook newsfeed digest i've stumbled upon your old dada surrealist reviews and thought - why not outdada the dada – and so i wrote this poem":

203
lightbulb wrestling sponge
- written on some beige fibreglass "peddle":
- off
ironing the guitar's long leg...

the one containing "flagged" rubber dripping a moving sepia
Annihilating
orange glove
striped grey
- drying the leg scarf designed electric greasy thong...

Oh...

Nothingness stuck with the glued vegetable giraffe painting the baguette of chaos
on the camoflage bandage

J.M. Bennett & O. Lindsann

Gut Bucket Research. *Nos. 4-7 (c.2010-19) ed. David Tigh. 799 Whitehill Way NE / Calgary, AB / T1Y 3E8 / Canada / uthar@hotmail.com.*

This is only one of several great unique periodicals published by David Tighe in Alberta; I'll be reviewing some others (*No Quarter & I Want an Army out of Caves*) in issues of *Rêvenance* and the *in-Appropriated Press*. It's an incredibly fun, esoteric, meticulously intellectual little TLP-sized zine that focuses on sound, primarily off the beaten track vocal sound – by way of example, one of the issues I have is dedicated to interspecies music, one to the work of William Corliss, a kind of Charles Fort of music, and one issue entitled "How Did Arthur miles Learn to Throat Sing? And other mysteries." There's a related zine (apparently not technically an issue of *Gut Bucket...*) to Eefing, yodeling, throat singing and "hollerin" (with side forays into people doing free improv jaw harp and kazoo?!). All of this from a perspective deeply rooted in avant-garde, heretical, and antinomian anarchist traditions that brings together the archaic, the experimental, and the potential applications and experiences of the voice as a vehicle for transforming realities. Get in touch and pick some of these babies up – then start making some noise!

– reviewed by Olchar E. Lindsann

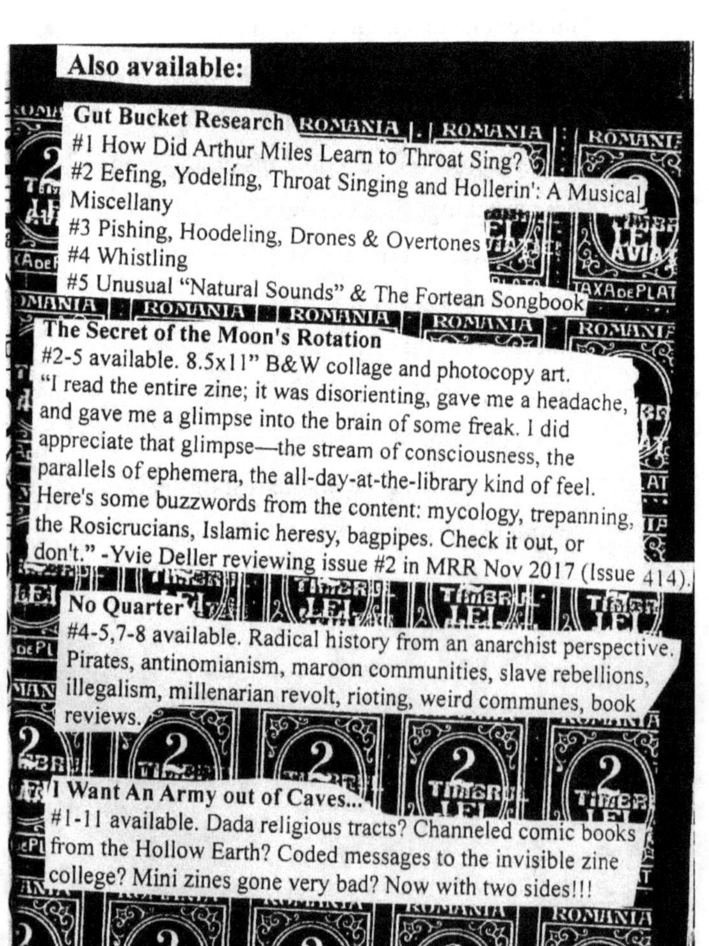

hands crossed, mouth open

Right

One / Two / Three

Agape, we perform
whether the affection is proper or improper

c.o.r.r.e.c.t
/ correct

a portion of depressed hair has fallen down

"Place"

Not airy but hairy

One / Two

a.g.a.i.n
/ again

A quadrille, advancing two steps
& self-regulating

Back

He reads correctly when he likes.

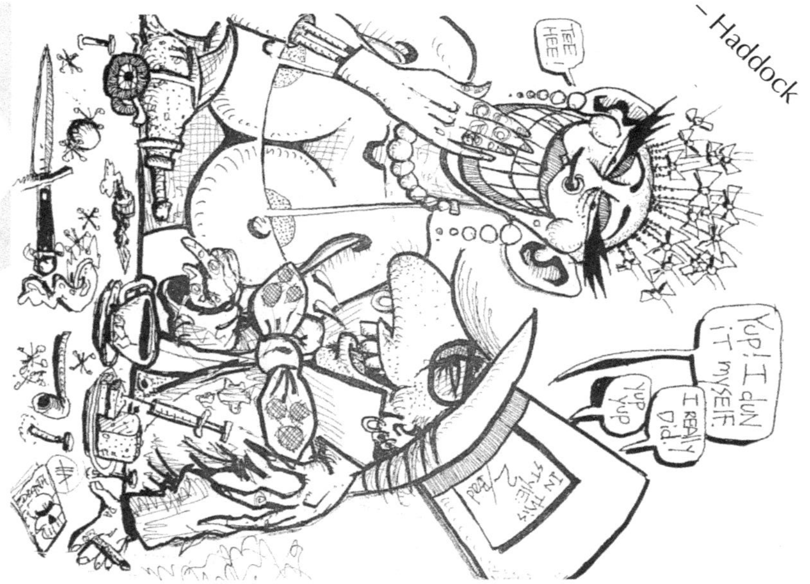

– Haddock

– Musicmaster

Above: *Mark Leahy, from* threaded insert. *'threaded insert' consists of a series of instructions, for orientation, for steps, for speech, and other actions including spelling. These instructions are randomly selected from a database of short MP3 files. The content derives from guides and instructions for 'proper' speech, rules for social, sexual and public conduct, and the control or modification of the body. 'threaded insert' can happen anywhere, but in performance the work brings attention to qualities and features of its particular location.*

wolf ganglion

Oodles of gobs and flecks of slaver dangling from the jut of strident jouncing turbulent "must." Hassle free "must" embedded with beat sticks what have learnt to whistle. Tunelessly.

*

*

*

Seltzer arrives in a neat squirt. Fit subject for librettos or the stuff of nightmares. Gastronomic eye balls dangle from fundamental nylon runs. Blink in perpetuity.

– William Repass

The horse and buggy—a Central Park tradition

A pretzel vendor on every corner...

New York taxis—the cheapest thrill in town

The New York Stock Exchange

Central Park—New York's oasis

– found poem from Tom Cassidy

One Moment in July

I did not argue him away from his affection. I left off thought
and let it be awhile, this arduous July of heat and friction
and desire for coolness if some smoothing could evolve.

He was asking my agreement, and my voice relaxed
into professional response, conveying maybe
that opinions matter less than what we build between us,

part intentional and part an accident in openness.
How is everyone important independently? The space between
one voice and another cradles something in us wanting

to be played the way a violin or game of handball might,
with every facet of being intertwined with
every facet of being known and almost loved.

Because that's what we do when we allow the softness
spirited and clear and gentling toward a picture
that includes the roses and the nutrients and land and breath and sky.

– Sheila E. Murphy

The Sacred Conspiracy:

The Internal Papers of the Secret Society of Acéphale and Lectures to the College of Sociology

ed. Marina Galletti and Alastair Brotchie. 2018. London: Atlas Press.

Reviewed by Olchar E. Lindsann

The work of Georges Bataille is by no means unknown in the English-speaking world, but with the publication of *The Sacred Conspiracy: The Internal Papers of the Secret Society of Acéphale and Lectures to the College of Sociology*, the scope, depth, and radically uncompromising nature of his full praxis has finally become available to us, a project chillingly resonant and uncomfortable (sometimes problematic) in the way that our current epoch demands. Editors Marina Galletti and Alastair Brotchie have arranged a mosaic from a wealth of rare and newly revealed documents that chart the public and the occult face of Bataille's most intimate and essential collective endeavor, in the years leading up to the outbreak of World War II: the College of Sociology, a definitively *anti*-academic group whose public lectures sought to radicalize the nascent field of Sociology in their series of public lectures, and the Secret Society of the Acéphale, which sought a new living myth to respond to the spiritual deprivation of Modernity whose anguish was being harnessed by emerging Fascism.

Though a number of his writings are available in translation, Bataille's image in anglophone circles has been dominated by the two most popular translations of his work: the hallucinatory sado-erotic *Story of the Eye,* and *The Accursed Share,* dealing with his theory of expenditure, a seminal work in the development of Critical Theory. There has been relatively little awareness of his deep involvement with the dense network of the pre-war avant-garde and radical political groupings and ventures – the cultural context and social forms through which his thought was developed. The result is a de-contextualized, fractured conception of his complex and closely-knit range of activity, obscuring the fact that the theoretical tradition now dominating the academies did not originate in the academy, but in coalitions of intellectuals working outside and against it. Several anthologies have sought to combat this oversight, including *The Absence of Myth,* ed. Michael Richards, and the *Encyclopaedia Acephalica,* published by Atlas Press.

It is important that *The Sacred Conspiracy* is also published on Atlas, whose catalog of translations and anthologies has done more than any other to shape the anglophone understanding of Pataphysics, Dada, Surrealism, Symbolism, and the French avant-Garde generally. And though Bataille is the focus here, the book opens onto an entire intellectual community almost unknown in English, with texts by over a dozen of his collaborators. We glimpse those peripherally as well as those directly involved with these organizations, suggesting an unknown constellation of thought, with short tantalizing biographical notices.

Today's ideological and cultural climate is ripe for this unveiling of that community's underlying project, which goes far beyond literature, theory, or even (they claimed) politics. On the eve of World War II, Acéphale diagnosed a social malaise of disintegration, in which the unifying symbols, mythologies, and communal rituals that bound individuals to each other and society – the domain of what Bataille designates as the Sacred – had been emptied of meaning. Religion, the domain traditionally addressed to the sacred, had failed its purpose, as had the secular religions of science and revolutionary politics that replaced it; Acéphale's conception of the sacred was built upon the myth of the Death of God, symbolized by the figure of the Headless Man.

Fascism, Bataille argued, appeals to the personal void thus created in individuals, offering a twisted image of the Sacred for which liberal democracy had failed to advance a viable alternative. Today, it would be laughable to suggest that we have since solved this problem, and our current descent into neo-fascism mirrors in a chilling fashion the trajectory played out beneath our eyes in the book's meticulous timelines. Too much of it feels horrifically familiar: the vague sense of dread and thwarted urgency, the helpless rage in the face of minor catastrophes accumulating more quickly than they can be digested or reacted to – everything, *perhaps*, but the persistent, guttering ghost of faith that a single effort by a committed group of mystical theorists might yet change the course of human destiny.

In the intervening eighty years, an assortment of factors have gutted the legitimacy of the ethical claims upon which that faith was based, and it will make the fervid, intellectually abstruse collective activity revealed here unfamiliar to most readers, while the very fact of its relative cultural visibility will surprise the rest. Although these communities still exist, they are exponentially more isolated from the main-stream of intellectual culture, and it is difficult to picture this kind of undertaking having any visibility at present, even while its necessity feels more inescapable as one proceeds through the collection.

All of this prompts the reader to question many terms whose sociopolitical definitions, oppositions, and implications we have come to take for granted – for instance "excess", the "political", the "sacrifice", and most importantly the "sacred." In these texts, some written for publication and others only for fellow initiates, the group explores the loss of the sacred in society and some possible, radical responses to it. These include individual meditation, secret societies and affinity groups such as Acéphale itself to counterbalance kinship affiliations and cement personal bonds between individuals, and the intersecting concept of Festival when the regulating hierarchies and taboos of society are temporarily suspended, bonding individuals to the whole society through shared moments of sacred ecstasy.

The relationship of expenditure to the Sacred that is elaborated in *The Accursed Share* and exhibited quite differently in *Story of the Eye* is reflected here in the emphasis on sacrifice. The necessity of sacrifice to the invocation of the Sacred was no mere metaphor for Bataille: his research culminated in a proposal that Acéphale perform a human sacrifice, offering himself as victim; nobody was willing to perform the killing.

It is easy enough to smirk at this; we do so at our peril. Without (obviously) endorsing human sacrifice, the fact that such absolute *commitment* to the most radical forms of communal resistance have become practically unthinkable in today's intellectual terrain should fill us with shame or horror, not derision. We must think twice before denying the power of sacrifice today, in the face of impending mass scarcity and the very real threat of fascist resurgence to power across the globe. These texts force us to face many such harsh propositions.

Problematics abound.

If Nietzsche makes you uncomfortable, so will Acéphale. Indeed, Zarathustra occupies a central place in their thought, and theirs is not a path of utopia, egalitarianism, or comfort. The Acéphale sometimes feels like an anarchic, Dionysian Super-Man, though they typically avoid that term. If we find the championing of Nietzsche simultaneously with the rise of Fascism unnerving, this was acknowledged by the group themselves; they were outspoken in their aim to rescue his ideas from the mis/interpretation of the Third Reich, and indeed the College was largely conceived to serve as an anti-fascist organization.

The impending war presented complex questions; for Bataille, war potentially represented a form of the healthy sacrifice of a civilization – a proposition that seems uncomfortably close to the fascist avant-garde of Marinetti, Pound, or Whyndam Lewis. But *this* was not a "healthy" war, and there is no hint of celebration anywhere in these pages. Ultimately Pierre Andler urged that members should be allowed to join the war effort as anti-nationalist anti-Fascists so long as "we continue to love and hate in war the things we chose and rejected in peace, and that we remember what unites us and what must unite so many others, all others."

Lest we become too ethically comfortable however, great reservations are also expressed here about democracy, or democracies – it is often unclear whether the target is democracy itself or the nation-states representing it. The condemnations of the democratic powers' hypocrisy and virtual oligarchy still ring true, but in the context of their time, as in ours, the ambiguity is unsettling, as was the group's eventual decision to withdraw from political activity as futile – albeit while continuing to lecture and publish explicitly against Fascism. The ideas of Caillois, Monnerot, and others in the group did indeed lead them to flirt with Fascism, anti-semitism and white supremacy – but all were pushed out of the group as soon as those tendencies began to emerge.

We find no answers here, though much insistence; the language pushes theoretical language to the verge of fervid hallucination, it is allusive and coy; it is mysticism, not philosophy, and must be read as such. The sea of conversations, shared readings, shared understandings, and interpersonal undercurrents in which these texts were eddies have long vanished. What is revealed is not an organized system or ideology or practice or plan, but a throbbing social *body,* awash with impulses, anguish and a bit of ecstasy, headless like the figure of the Acéphale itself, however the intellectual the form through which it expels its excess of thought.

So many apparent contradictions. A frenetic undercurrent of despair runs throughout all of the protestations of joy in chaos, a sense of inadequacy to the civilization's disaster throbs through their rhapsodies of virility. It was this despair, brought to a head at the moment of Bataille's proposal of human sacrifice – only hinted at obliquely in the documents, curtly confirmed long after Bataille's death by certain initiates – that precipitated the secret society's dissolution. Their faith in their power to stem the tide did not survive the war.

It is thanks to the inspiringly meticulous editing and annotation of the volume, something of a masterpiece of bibliography, that the full materiality of the group's praxis, enlaced as it was with daily life, comes through in such unrelenting fashion. Seventy-five pages of exhaustive and insightful introductory material situates the group in their cultural and historical contexts. They also offer an amusingly mysterious glimpse into the truly secret nature of Acéphale as they recount the decades-long tale of the compilation of these documents, which resembles an episode from an Umberto Eco mystery, complete with evasive witnesses and files quietly passed along at secret meetings in obscure cafés. Underscoring the historical grounding of the activity, the texts are organized into chronological sections, each introduced first with a day-by-day timeline of communications, activities, and publications of members as well as the international events that framed and inflected them, followed by the editors' detailed commentaries providing an intellectual history of the months in question as reflected in the anthologized texts. An elegant system of marginal bullets, easily learned, allows for fluid cross-referencing and identification of each document's origins.

Indeed, everything about the volume's presentation insistently grounds the group's activities firmly in its active, historical dimension, refusing a predictably abstract, essentially theoretical or ideological perspective. This responds to the primary concern of that generation, reflected by Acéphale, the Grand Jeu, the Surrealists, and many others – so distant from the central streams of creative culture today – that avant-garde textual production resist the seduction of falling back into "mere literature". It is only in this way, in which the matrix of the theoretical, the personal, the social and the political is constantly in view, that Acéphale can be discerned *as a society,* of which the texts are relics no more or less essential to the group's significance than any other aspect of their multifaceted lives and commitments.

It is in this dimension, more than on the levels of theoretical, literary, or even mythological production, that the collective *experience* of Acéphale – an experience which, as Bataille never tires of repeating, will likely break one's heart – should unsettle, disturb, needle us out of our skins. And whether to learn or to be warned, our discomfort should be vertiginous, like the future staring at us through its pages.

–Olchar E. Lindsann

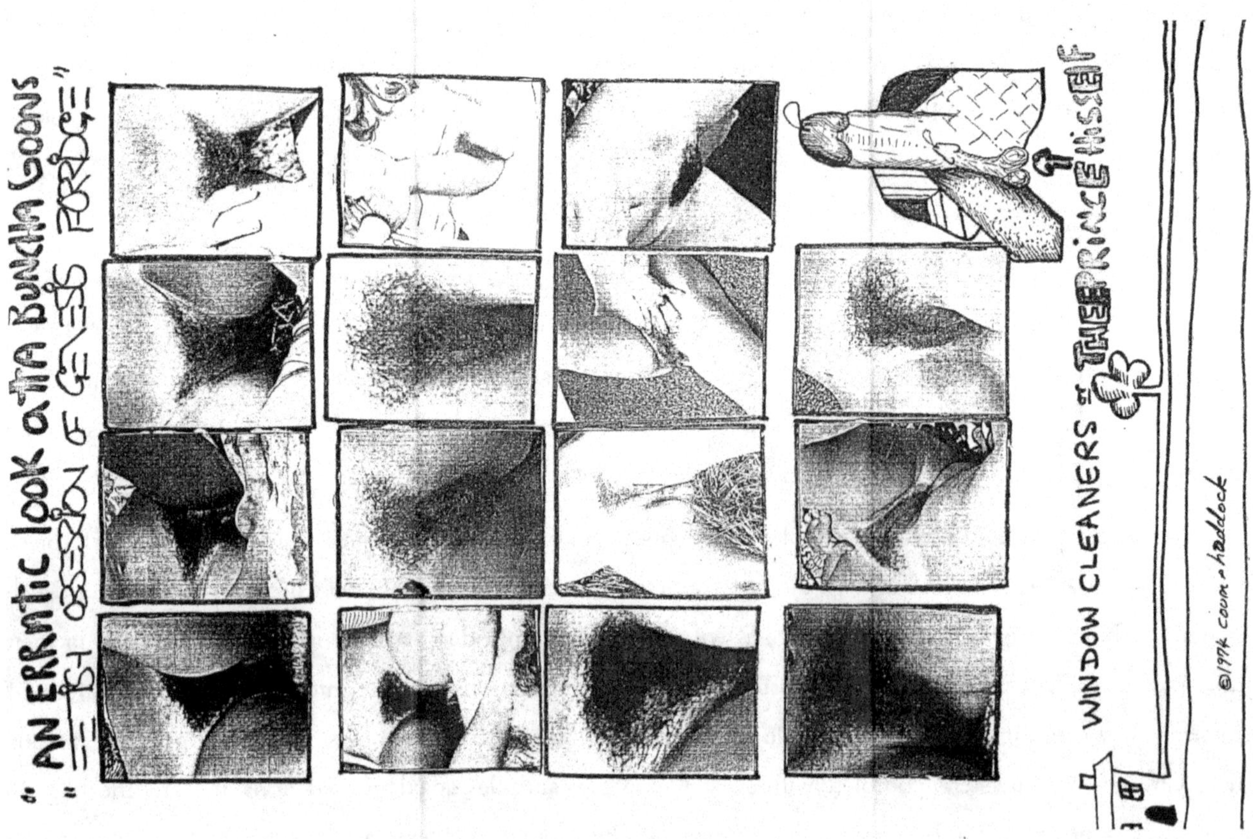

by Haddock & Genesis p-Orrige – ***R.I.P. Genesis, March 14, 2020***

INTENT

Your violently animated figure, a tally of infinite angles, views, and scopes; drunken flies of dry Jesu ejaculated with a gloomy appointment: an abortion made using the devil's 'shaving' money to entice these fractal sabers of illegal copulation. Our superior conflicts veil worms and prevent them from communicating precise thoughts. Man as a temporal impediment; thus, the machine and these offended, normalized, numb fingers. Death in style: TREES, roots, water, blood, rites, ideas, imagination, the neural branches, the vague grapeshot of a demonic stamp...AND you find a social way out of bleeding, as you must. Everything is a coded morgue. The senses shocked the senses outward beyond the possible, and WE turn to stop; yes, WE turn to stop as the convoluted processes weep into sub-ordered thought, thought with pathetically diminished intent; and each icy whore pools my mind into data-dumps of self-regulated genocide. Because I am more than 1 person. I am parasites and hosts. I auto-destruct for the smiling viewers within the blemished glass towers of my buried, celestial mind. And all of these lovely snuff viewers are my lovely snuff selves. They love to see me suffer. And in my suffering, they suffer as well, but they enjoy it as much as I do not. But where do my selves penetrate my sliced open, vivisected self? where, in fact, do we merge to Become?

I just love wrapping my long legs around my fucking minds. I love my channels to be corrupted and universally fucked. "Fuck Love" because love is being fucked as much and as often as my selves can provide. Thus, the more I suffer, the more I die, the more I become a multiplicity; and the more I become a multiplicity, the more I become a union.

Everything is the same when the head spins too quickly, when there is no rest...

– AG Davis

THE LAST ONE STANDING

The last one standing is the first one sitting

The first one sitting is the last one quitting

The last one quitting is the first bull shitting

The first bull shitting is the last one knitting

The last one knitting is the first Walter Mitting

The first Walter Mitting is the last epileptic fitting

The last epileptic fitting is the first pierced clitting

The first pierced clitting is the last arm pitting

The last arm pitting is the first fist hitting

– Bradley Lastname

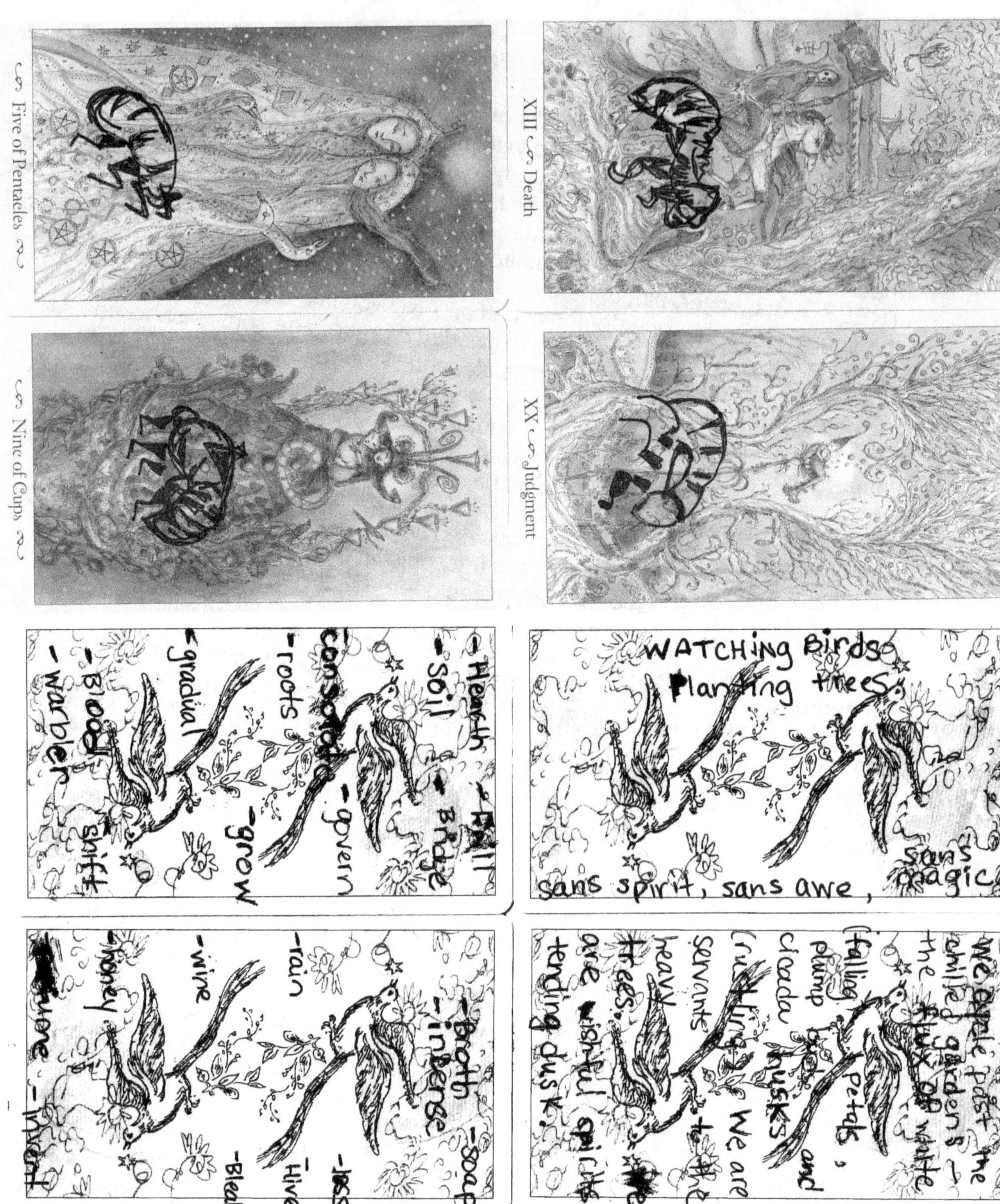

— *i. engine*

LIONS AND TIGERS AND BEARS OH MY

Lufthansa and Southwest and Lot, let's fly
Apple and pumpkin and mince, eat pie
Chop onions and shallots and leeks, then cry
Boardwalk and Park Place and Baltic, you'll buy
Molly and blotter and kush, get high
Nooses and cyanide and glocks, you die

– *Bradley Lastname*

He was obviously a ranking Bozo, and I addressed him jokinglyas a fool. His arms waved, he hopped from foot to foot for emphasis. With nobody watching, with nobody listening. I almost went into hysterics. At that moment I wanted above all else to have my parents beside me, so that I could blot out the light. Time in the conventional sense lost its meaning. There was only a time out at a tavern on Friday nights to mix moderate drinking with heavy thinking.

Then my new-found friend dipped a glass into the jar and handed it to me with a grin. It's a sixth sense, for watching the face of the man you deal with, especially if he's one of the Bozos, a people known for their skilled optimism, but as classic clowns and villains. The people rebelled. Their only weapon was their overwhelming numbers. They probably would float, rising and falling with the swells. I could see the reason for their evident determination to remain exactly where they returned to shore for more magic. Their leader performed a ritual, throwing stones, to appease the resident spirit, the blood of a otherworldly voice was instantly compelling.

The Bozos showed me a fish equipped to potsmoking pipes conditions. This species of a sub waxin haddock, was said to drink heavily must run to the post office The fish transmits informationof the bawdyart arrive in the mail. Thus anchored, the haddock was often drunk, sought companionship by talking to stones or pieces of driftwood, or by capturing insects and breathing on them until they grew as large as human beings, and so could serve as mail artist friends. Somehow these fishes can talk and order more beer, will become silent, stare into space, so huff and a puff of weed

The Bozos, however, doubted my explanation of the fish's Mail works of art.

"They're trash fish," one old-timer told me with disgust. "So full of bones I'd as soon eat when one is drunk." For a moment I explored my jacket pocket I found a ribbon of paper, my fortune-cookie message from the evening's dinner. It said, "Fuck You, . . ."

– *The Haddock*

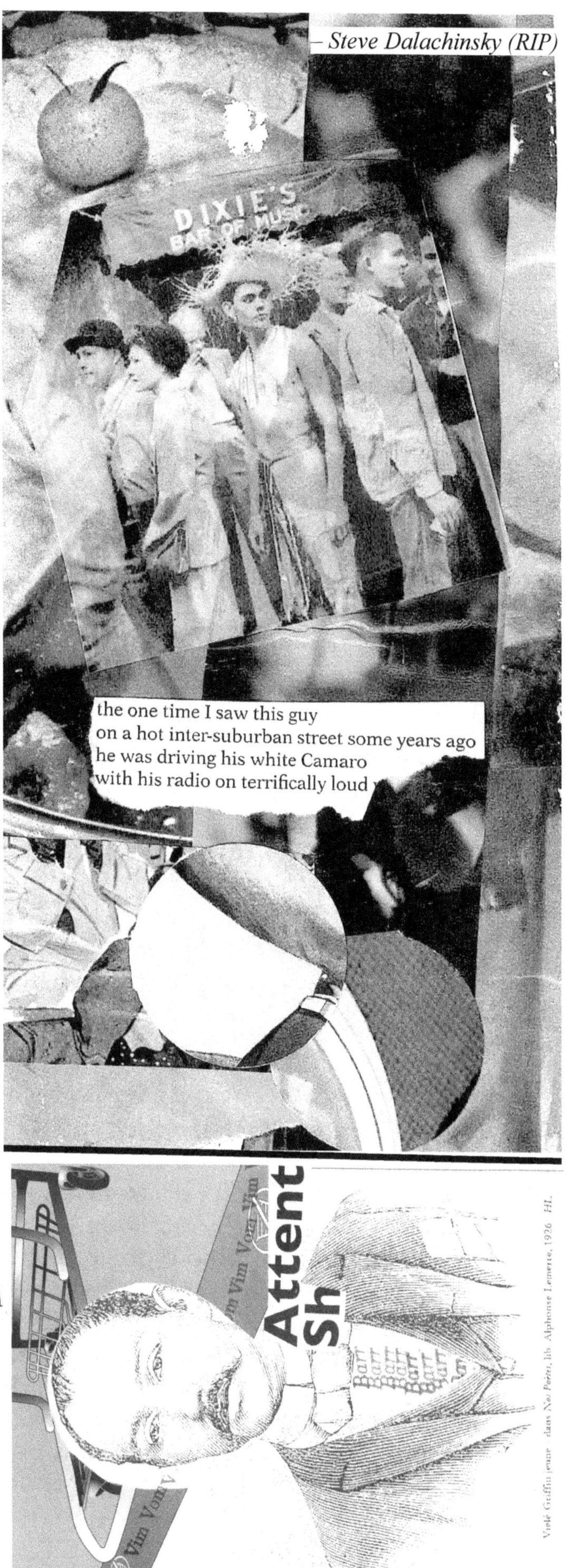

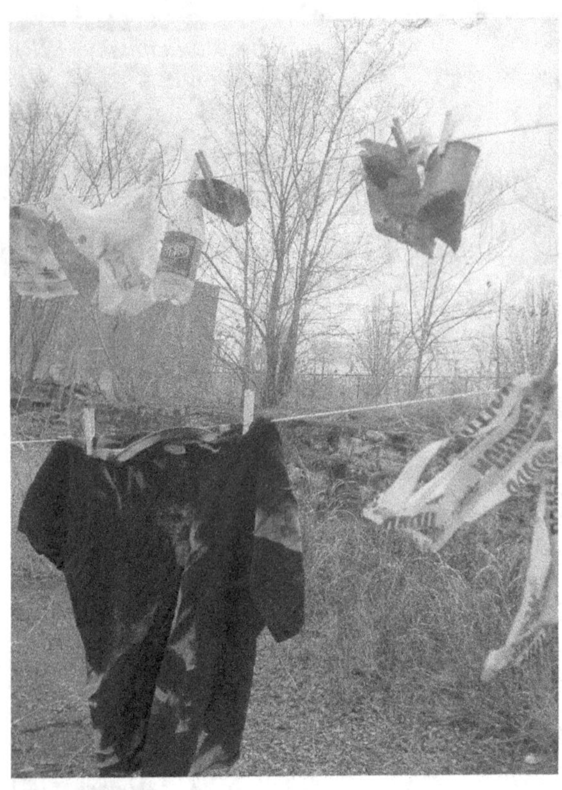

Jennifer Weigel
Cast Off

interactive outdoor clothesline installation featuring detritus found on site and hung to the line with clothespins

installed during:
Artica, St. Louis, Dec. 2009
Art for the Earth, The Gardens at SIUE, Edwardsville, Apr. 2010

Weathered and worn,
floating on the wind,
tattered, forgotten, abandoned
testaments to human existence.
Archeology is a gateway to the past,
good, bad and ugly…
Always remember:
we learn about our history and ourselves
from our trash as well as our treasures.
What record are we leaving behind?

Preda Tory Vic Tory
on the election results of
*Friday the 13*th*, 2019.*

hatecloud glowerd
woe ô albion
cap-sized lection licking
woundes
albion alas
scuttled isle weeply weaking
shame albion
barque by bigots barnacled
albion jaundice in
fected, briganded by
selfly ship of foolscap
albion for
lorn adrift in fascististic
fester, fost'ring poison
freezeth albion
comatose in fundhouse-mirror
of the bastard-bortion
america america its seep of evil
drifting back to its birthplace
purge
welcome with us woe ô albion
albion of almost
albion i love who suicides
an albion i loved

–Olchar E. Lindsann

HOT TOPIC

2020 version: I Support Black Lives Matter

Musical Instructions

1. One sound after another (of different lengths) mainly quietly.

2. If sounds coincide (by accident) the other players should deliberately try to coincide one more sound before going back to the instruction.

3. Occasionally, some long sounds may overlap.

4. Throughout the performance an extra performer should read a current political text, newspaper account or the like. This performer should read their text in a neutral mezzo-forte voice, at a medium speed. This may or may not be done with a microphone. Right wing texts are not allowed.

There should be pauses of varying lengths between paragraphs.

Note: The subtitle of this piece should change according to whatever progressive causes are current.

Sam Richards 2011/20

Elysian Fields of Power

(For Stephanette, Ivana eventually)

So, Tiny Tom and Speedy Gonzales
Have had a Lab,
It was pretty much a physical thing,
They tried to outdo the topology of a body in space
From person A to person B ran the 'power-field of
a person', so, how would we envelope them
into our power-circle, if we were to say
'I'm taking over a situation'?
then
You would say 'I don't want to take a person
In my power-field, I want them to be free,
And besides, I'm not Pina Bausch or Vito Acconci',

Documentation is more a referent than a remainder
And performance means
There's an audience,
An event is an accident sometimes
And sometimes it's steady and sleepy, like a video;
There may be people or not
A couple of technical by-products
But what always really counts is people
Who make decision whether
to be there or not to be
as we're making a private
out of their public space
and
not everyone can get it…
we are just trying to become these buildings
themselves, a part of the architectural landscape,
surroundings which is
the other

—Nina Zevoncevik

Sooner or later those character deficiencies are going to get the better of you. You need someone like me to iron them out.

JETSON

~~~~~~~~~~~~€~~~~£~₩?~~

"strafe tyrants with a metal ruler, har har"
- Gerard the Nervous, Substantially Substandard (1622)

~~~~~~~~~~~~~~~~~~^oo^~~~o

"tuition FREE? Yu should live so long, grasshopper"
- L.J. Letterbox (2321)

÷~÷~÷~○●○●○●○●○

jestson, jettison planet of my dreams with appetite reptilian (?) It's a snake eating its damn tail
great snakes dig tropic oil crab conversion charts
senseless dingo on ice rinkydink which one melts better?
treasure talk alone fused spinal space in ringworm on
Hupitor (3rd sun from our the)
kill the sap before reproduction jibberjabber
phlegmish ice clock in oven
ô hock shop ö
don't dig
Œô squid liver we don't space nor drop skylab from inversion
glitch square development
burn the back 40 the fallow m'oor/off/
expanse in with reemergence oppression
statins back stardoom a common cold flotation deride and pollen hates a vacuum
feckless crash course upstream, dome of mirror-shoed nation of ballcocks
("who plugged thine commode plunged thy soul")
dig - this is tiresome

– Michael Dec, after Lindsann, "Jettison"

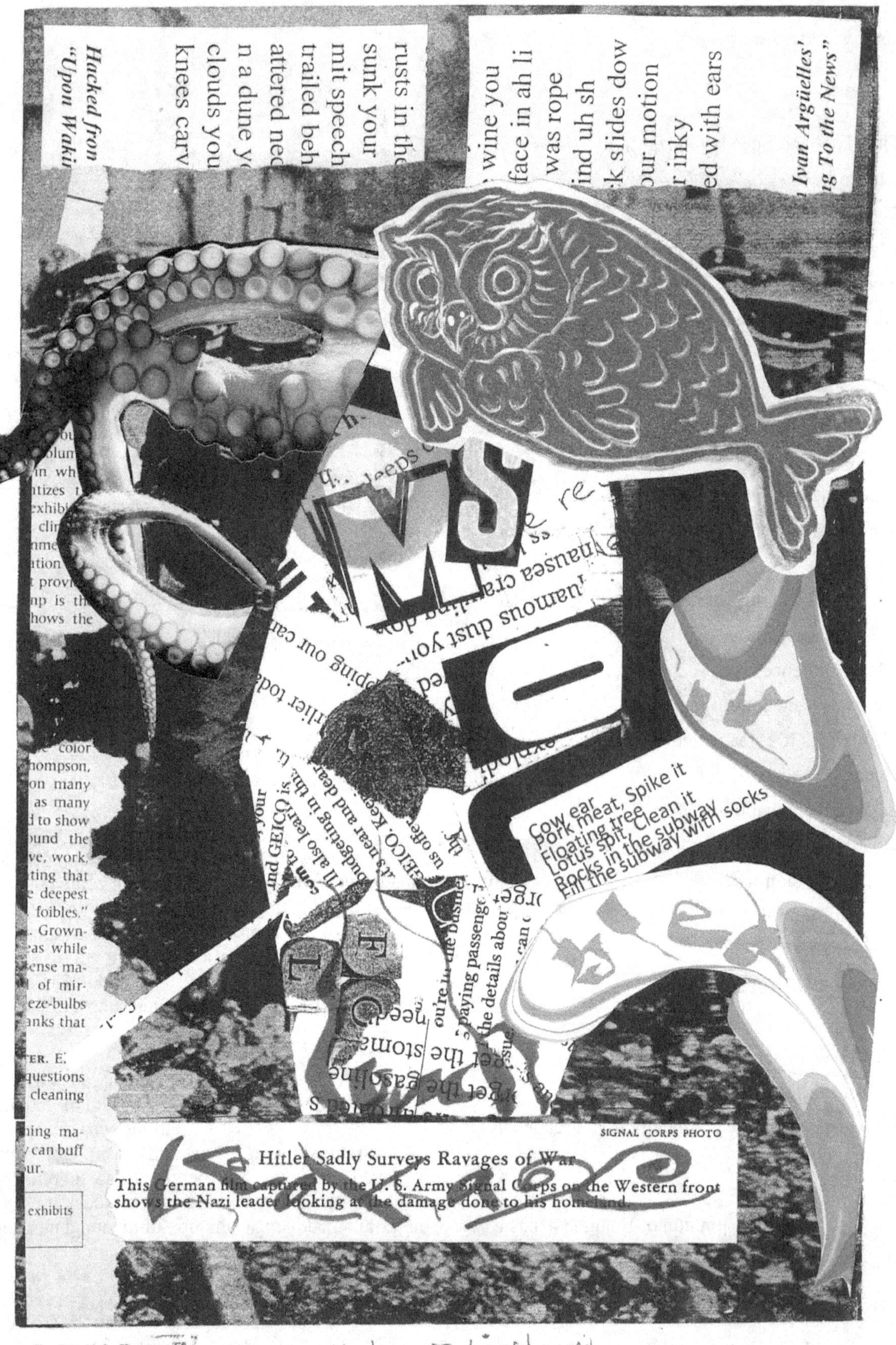
OWL FISH
Cow ear
Pork meat, Spike it
Floating tree
Lotus spit, Clean it
Rocks in the subway
Fill the subway with socks
Hitler Sadly Surveys Ravages of War
SIGNAL CORPS PHOTO
This German film captured by the U. S. Army Signal Corps on the Western front shows the Nazi leader looking at the damage done to his homeland.
C. Mehrl Bennett
Olchar E. Lindsann
JOHN M. BENNETT

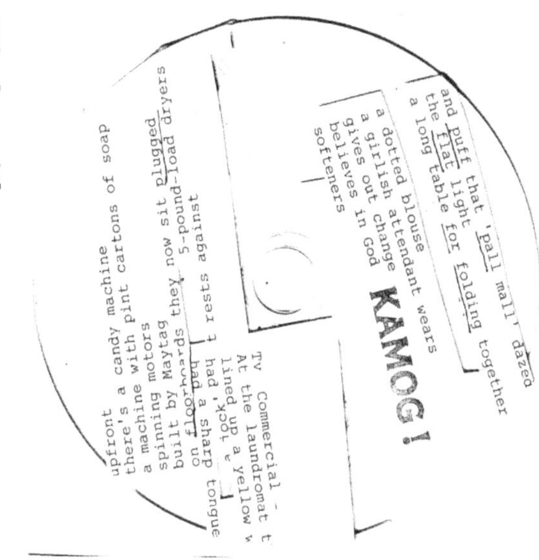

– Jessy Kendall, Mark Sonnenfeld & O. Lindsann

Dia-logarithm

Tact cuts off the oxygen he said
Miracles are effete she said
Contrite yourself to depths he said
Bowl me over something plain she said
Beneath the epidermis all corruption shows he said
Bracketed lilies are still lilies she said
Campsites differ from campesinos he said
Lamp light deflects my innocence she said
Water every liberty you knew he said
Fault lines disappear until they don't she said
Reminiscence baked in means indelible defection he said
Sparkling roses shadow matt finish roses she said

– Sheila E. Murphy

now a beak heaper

it was the pollen in the burlap bag that saved us

calcium bone was the lead guitarist

combined itch was the fullback that year

it takes a lion to head off the musical ghosts

we're all going to the bowling alley to play darts

– J.D. Nelson

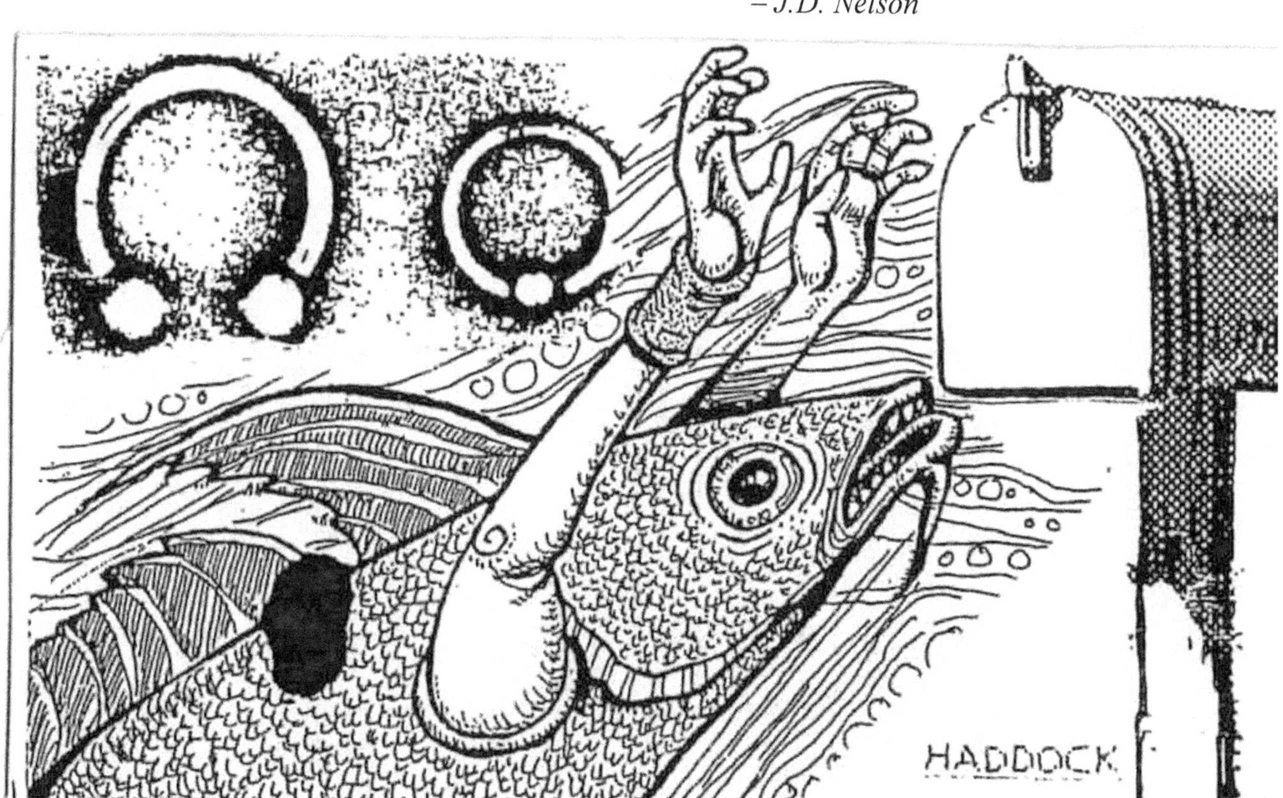

Nothing if not well organized for games of skill. But as for chance? Smile, dentures—miss! Splenetic lather confused with glue—miss! Horse shoes champ bit as the phalanx, breast plated w/ bronze nipples, squelches forward in tight formation across the mud flats. Termagant the insult, or maybe ptarmigan, bowled at this entity. To a cartoon bean pole, horse shit was the preemptive response. The scenery changed and so did our essence. Calque got all over our patent leather dermis and we no longer went out of an evening to throw dice or rouse rabble. The rough element saw a horse shoe flash before minds' eye with a resounding clank. You must admit, the physics are glitchy and not well stimulated. Well, neither is the dialogue. Flambeurs like Bob or Dostoevsky squinting down the distant hob.

– William Repass

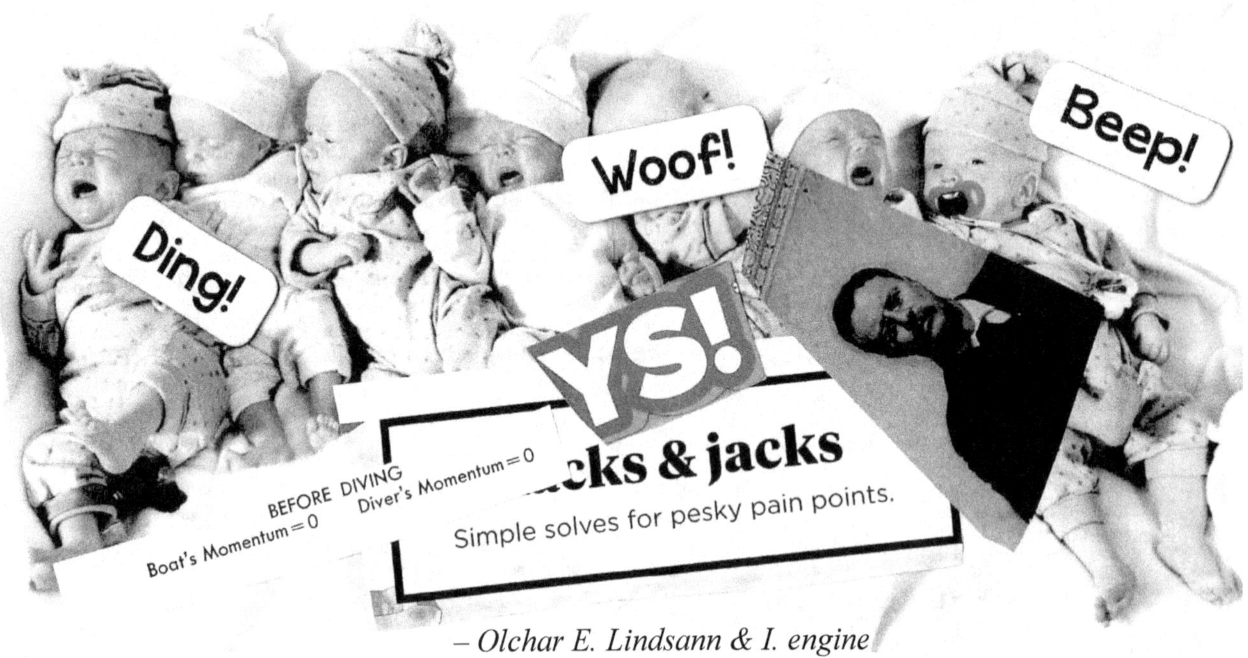

– Olchar E. Lindsann & I. engine

metal then arrived

metal then arrived gave breast armpits
not smoke stole bat Tulan moved eat
name came passes blood dark prick sun
good then pierced face sleep honor
swell mountain gathers bottom food
passed through drink maize therefore
stones on sand borne faster top dawn
spoils search back Jaq'awitz mountain
crowded hidden dawn vipers bowels
passed through changed trembles
flat moss hearts forest dawns
face incense glitters wept copal
pumas wings soggy person mirror
within its hiding self biting moon
hearts burned burial then appeared
weeping Yaki trouble change speech
house placed heart mountain difference

De-reading the Popol Vuh – 20
–John M. Bennett

LEATHER NUN LAMENTS

by Scott MacLeod

1.

A young woman sleeps in a small airplane flying high over the clouds, dreaming of an old woman living in a tiny house on a tiny island in the Devil's Sea, far below. Caught in the blinding flash of the sun, the airplane flies on, surfing the clouds. A single buoy clangs somewhere below, out at sea.

The young woman in the airplane is fleeing the fictions of doubt and pleasure. Her patient sleep appears as a meteor in this context, and delivers her subjective body to nothing. Draped in black mourning, never uttering a sound, the old woman on the island is fleeing this void too, by cutting, sewing, treading, seeding. From time to time she lifts her black veil and paces down to the water's edge, spits into the Devil's Sea and climbs back up to her cabin on the rocks, dropping her veil and recovering her poise.

2.

The ocean is like gelatin. Then a splinter of blue light at the center of the picture. We hear a symphony of underwater sounds: landslide, metabolic sounds, the rare and secret noises that certain undersea species share with each other.

Her expression freezes. The water-lump is racing for her. It bolts her upright, out of the water to her hips, then slams her hard, whipping her in an upward arc of eight feet before she is jerked down to her open mouth. Another jolt, down to her floating hair. One hand claws the air, fingers trying to breathe, then it, too, is sucked below in a final and terrible jerking motion. Hold on the churning froth of a whirlpool until we are sure it is over.

Moral: There's no such thing as a free lunch.

3.

The snap of a twig breaks the young woman's sleep, brings her up out of her airplane dream like a white shark to the surface of the sea. The young woman (let's call her Blossom) sees a strange red mist hovering slowly and suspiciously over the wreckage of a white Cessna. She draws back her arrow and, holding the bow in front of her, walks towards the mist as it begins to take the form of a human figure. Great is her surprise when the mist speaks to her.

"I have lived on this island for many years, cursed by an evil witch, who banished me here from the sea and the skies. Since then, I have been wandering around, neither here nor there, stuck in the in-between. I used to be a fisherman, and have been longing for a chance to return to the sea."

The mist-figure has magically grown, twice as large as her tiny shack. The old woman steps back in fear, as the misty figure slowly begins to solidify. It curses itself for what it is about to do.

4.

All is quiet, not a breath of wind. Then a splinter of crimson light at the center of the picture. The gun barrels' strobe lights pop into the foreground, close by, and the night breaks wide open. Two women stride out from a tremendous gullet, from the onrushing undersea world at night. They head toward the mist-creature (we'll call it Orca), carving neon red phosphorescence into the air as they move. Their weapons make musical sounds in the night as they circle the Orca, weaving phosphorescence around it like a fishing basket. The night skies, the silent waters are now alive in dancing light.

Popping open in the short summer night, cherry bosoms blossom.

5.

Alright, alright. Look, I put the God damn dress on alright? I think I'm handlin' myself with a little bit of fuckin' restraint. While your zealous idealism disgusts me! I mean you got me chained up here like I'm some kind of dog! Collar YOUR dog!

6.

Blossom's eyes adjust to the darkness and she looks around. There is gear everywhere in the old woman's hut. The walls are adorned with dried shark hides, coiled ropes dangle like serpents above a galley stove that leaks smoke and holds two weeks worth of filthy dishes. Copper tubes, wooden barrels, bamboo rods, homemade harpoons, an antique knife collection and a dizzy array of shark hooks line the walls, with one entire wall dedicated to a collection of shark jaws, from the blue shark to the Great White. In the center of this orifice of decay, we see the Orca hunched over an iron tub of steaming oils.

7.

From below we see a fish-eye view, the outlines of swimmers, of people lying on rafts, arms and legs dangling tantalizingly in the blue water. A pair of feet kicking and arms paddling produces bizarre underwater vibrations, louder than human ears would normally perceive.

8.

Open your eyes, princess! Restraint? Ideals? Ideals can only be spoken by those powerful enough to carry them out. And that excludes you! Your weakness is a sin. You're a beautiful animal... and I'm weak, and I want you.

9.

The Orca sits on unruffled waters under a planetarium of star-life alive overhead with shooting stars every now and again making incisions into the heavens and leaving green trails behind. Many ships and planes have mysteriously disappeared in this area, possibly because of magnetic variations. Angels banished from heaven have no choice but to become devils.

You're all shook up, aren't you, baby?

10.

The mist-creature's appearance shimmers between Orca, its true self, and The Old Woman, its most recent, and still unresolved, incarnation. Like one of those lenticular postcards, tilted one way you see the Sphinx and tilted the other you see Cleopatra. Blossom thinks she might also see something like a bulldog in the shadows behind the iron tub, licking.

11.

Blossom allows her eyes to descend to the level of representation, into the nets of confident beauty, the top of her body slowly verbalizing both the murmur and the visual sequence. Orca holds out a jar of HUMUNCULUS beer to calm Blossom down. Here baby, pop the top before you blow your own!

12.

Blossom grabs the bottle with both hands, fits her pink lips around the gaping orifice tight like rubber gaskets and drains it dry in long, deep-throated gulps. Once you taste poison, you might as well finish the meal.

13.

... trickling from a village child's sleeve ... cherry blossoms ... pouring onto the faces of sinners ... cherry blossoms ... about 13 year olds sitting on the table ... staring at me without moving or blinking and all wearing black and I was rolling a dutch tulip ... I really got scared dropped the tulip wasted the mix ran inside ... I've seen the walls melting and everything just started to get dark and I got lost inside well I thought I was lost

14.

Let's closely examine this evil creation, this new breed encased and contained within the supple skin of woman. The softness is here, the unmistakable smell of female, the surface shiny and silken, the body yielding yet wanton. But a word of caution: handle with care and don't drop your guard. Even the devil in her sometimes loses her horns ... cherry blossoms scatter.

15.

This rapacious new breed prowls both alone and in packs, operates at any level, any time, anywhere, and with anybody. Who are they? One might be your secretary, your doctor's receptionist... or a dancer in a go-go club!

16.

What are you doing? Why do you run? You still have not called me. Face forward. You should be able to hear it now. That which blocks your ears is worthless fear. What is there to fear? Cast off your fear. Look forward! Go forward! Never stand still. Retreat and you will age. Hesitate and you will die. Shout ... my name is ... Orca!

17.

Blossom follows a precise path through Orca, touching centers of light and dark spots while she moves forward. Orca the warrior finds innovation and antiquity in the task of urban cleansing and seizes the air and dust, the ghosts, machines, architectures and symbols that bring forth a space of clarity. All those who enter this clear space, for instance Blossom, will live as an initiatrix: a woman so disfigured by crashes that she's forced to wear a mask.

18.

You want me to kill Blossom? Don't be stupid! Seventy million viewers, ma'am! They're all watching! Blossom can't die! After all, she's just a mask!

19.

Cherry Blossom! Cherry Blossom the legend, Cherry Blossom the indestructible! Sole survivor of the titanic pile-up of '95! Ripped up, wiped out, battered, shattered, creamed, and reamed... a dancer on the brink of death... Cherry Blossom, who lost a leg in '98, an arm in '99! With half a face and half a chest, and all the guts in the world, she's hanging on for dear life!!

20.

Let me lure you to me. Let me brush your hand aside. Let me wind my slender arm around your neck. Let my fingers descend the mountain. A mood sets in.

21.

Let me suck the fever from your parched lips.

22.

Let me....

23.

Cherry Blossom opens her eyes bound under the mist creature Orca. Welcome to violence, Cherry Blossom. Both word and act, cloaked a plethora of disguises, violence devours all it touches, its voracious appetite rarely fulfilled. Yet violence doesn't only destroy, it creates and molds as well.

I'd like a big-tittie girl to lick peanut butter off my toes.

That ain't gonna happen. That car is not gonna start.

24.

Three hundred pounds of torque with sequential multi-port fuel injection. Hit the kill switches!

Her dangling sleeve, her flowing long black hair made to punish men for their sins! Extravagant Spring calls to awaken a young girl, Blossom blossoms through the teeth of her comb. Barely a man! His sutras toppled!

25.

Nothing worse than being strong, but not strong enough.

26.

And you shall shed tears of scarlet.

27.

My skin is so soft. It pains me to see it touched by a corrupt world in its latter days, but: Cherry Blossom. Her holy scent caught in a gentle good night.

28.

Give me your hand, Sister. It's the last lap. We can win this. Why won't this son of a bitch just die? If fate is a millstone, then we are the grist. There's nothing we can do except wish for strength. If I cannot protect them from the wheel, then give me a strong blade!

29.

Orca leans over the cauldron, through the rising mist, whispers to the Old Woman:

"Sister, you spout your words of wisdom while the current of my blood runs hot beneath my soft skin. Don't you miss touching it?"

30.

The Old Woman sighs: "All I can do is think about you and miss all your kisses like the spring. If only I had a sign that one day you'd be mine again, oh if I could hold you right then as the chill in this season sputters and spits and dies...."

31.

Droplets fall from a young girl's hair.

32.

"Beneath the shadows of heaven I have lifted the veil. I have created life, wrested the secret of life from death. Now do you understand? From the lives of those who have gone before, I have created life!"

33.

Orca the smoke monster's indeterminacy coalesces and hardens into adamantine sweetness, heartless cruelty, and voluptuous wanton purity. By contrast, sentimentality is pornographic.

34.

Cherry Blossom snaps off wild roses, slides them into my hair. She is weary and done with waiting.

The Old Woman will forever remember her howling down from that mountain:

"I am the wound and the knife, the limbs and the rack, the victim and the executioner!

You ask 'What will come into my burning lips?' I answer... 'The blood from my little finger.' "

35.

Later she lay congealing on grass, giving birth to a butterfly, in the country of spring.

The whole field would have been drenched to a scarlet with the blood the girl must have lost.

36.

The Orca goes down on her knees and bends over me, fairly gloating. There is a deliberate voluptuousness that is both thrilling and repulsive, and as it arches its neck it actually licks its lips like an animal. I can feel the soft, shivering touch of the lips on the super-sensitive skin of my throat, and the hard dents of two sharp teeth, just touching and pausing there.

37.

Someone once asked me, did I think I was the best future for my little girl? Something I've thought about for a long time. This is what I decided. No one in this world is perfect. Heaven knows I'm not. But I love her more than anyone else possibly could. In the end, that's all that matters. She's my chance at something else. Something better. And there's no way I'm letting go of that.

38.

My thick wild hair, its thousand strands, my heart disheveled, torn apart and my blood burns.

39.

Sorrow violently sweeps everything off the island, shakes the yellow leaves from the trees, pulls up the rotten roots. The Orca and the Old Woman want Cherry Blossom to change back into what she always had been. Everyone wants to see Cherry Blossom again. She moves them. Inspires them. And in this world, that's not so easy to come by.

40.

What does death mean to the bourgeoisie? Merely a sensitivity and sentimentality that is usually soggy, insipid, vaguely whining and reeking of trumped-up nostalgia.

41.

I will not insult you by trying to tell you that one day you will forget.

42.

You must not be frightened if a sadness rises up inside you larger than any you have ever felt; if a restiveness, like light and cloud shadows, passes through your hands and into all you do. You must believe that something is happening in you, that life has forgotten you, that it will let you fall.

43.

Get away from her, you bitch!

44.

As I wake, you tenderly shake my disheveled hair. There are stains on my shirt from a couple hours out with the boys. Just a couple hours out with the boys, and all memory has left my bones. There's blood on my teeth from what they did here. All good things come to an end. And me stumbling out of my heart.

45.

And now she is on top of the mountain, with the blood streaming down, terrible, nasty, dirty, but looking beautiful and elegant, lying there voluptuous, pure, good, totally giving, self-sacrificing, sexually sick, very physical, very muscular, and opinionated, but not in a pushy kind of way. And at the end she says, 'Leapin' Lizards!'

46.

Each stroke of Orca's tongue rips off skin after successive skin; all the skins of Cherry Blossom's life in the world slip off like fireflies, pulled by the wind, drifting away into the blue night, leaving behind a patina of shining hairs.

47.

Yeah, you should taste her majesty
My lil' cherry blossom
Just like a crow, it cut my throat
Yeah, you should taste my lil' cherry blossom
My lil' cherry blossom - Yeeeah
My lil' cherry blossom - Yeeahh
Oh yeah now
She's all right now
Yeeeaahh

48.

A old woman wakes up in a tiny house on a tiny island, dreaming of a young woman in a small airplane flying overhead far above the clouds. The young woman in the airplane is fleeing her own restless ardor. The sunlit sky is featureless and bright and the day is long but she snaps off wild roses. She closes her eyes like petals and falls asleep again. The airplane flies on, oblivious.

49.

The long day lengthens, gets brighter at higher and higher altitudes. Pain, or the memory of pain, is sucked away literally removed by something nameless until only a void is left. Pain turns finally into emptiness. Fly on, oblivious.

50.

Flying into the sun, the young girl slumbers on within the shelter of heightened dreams. Or at least she wants to believe that she is dreaming, and that she will awaken in a moment to see an awful knife descending toward her heart.

51.

Waiting impatiently for her lover she exposes her loose hair, which becomes entwined in the jungle vines. Her love for Orca and his poetic aspirations creates a unique bond between them, intensely erotic without being sexual. Suddenly a noise, like trolley cars in a dead city. There goes the baddest ass in the whole yard.

52.

She gently parts the shroud of mystery, revealing the flower, redder than red. She wants to apply his blood to her lips as lipstick but his blood is too dry.

53.

I am vampire of my own heart.

54.

Orca holds me close. "Spring doesn't last," I say to him.

"You don't believe in permanence, do you?"

"My skin is so soft." I picture myself stepping out of my bath into a Renaissance painting. I took his hands in mine, leading them to my young full breasts. Yesterday is another world, a thousand years away.

"What do you want?"
"Your blood all over me."

55.

Yet it rushes to me this minute! With your hand on my shoulder...

56.

Even angels get caught in the end with their halos round their throat.

57.

I see dead people.

58.

In the middle of the floor lay a skeleton, every vestige of flesh gone from the bones to which still clung the mildewed and moldered remnants of what had once been clothing. Upon the bed lay a similar gruesome thing, but smaller, while in a tiny cradle near-by was a third, a wee mite of a skeleton.

59.

"There are 3 reasons why you can't ever kill me. First, I'm better looking than you are. Second, your blows are too light. And third, there's nothing in the world I can't kill first."

60.

Let our hearts blow away somewhere, alone and alive where all the dark can't see.

61.

Moonlight flutters over a river of bones. The searchers keep searching for that lost airplane even in the fog and the dark. Like searching for a splinter in the soft meat where the thumb meets the palm.

62.

The old woman stirs a bubbling stew in its black pot. The darkest part of night has turned to snow and tumbles down onto the ground. She won't be surprised to find, in the morning, cherry blossoms on the roof of her hut.

63.

A young woman wakes in an airplane, at sea, caught in the blinding flash of the sun.

- - -

Source texts include:

Japanese fables & haikus
thetextasifsuch by Jim Leftwich
Jaws screenplay
Faster Pussycat Kill Kill screenplay
Manga & Anime quotes
Black Snake Moan quotes
Death Race 2000 script
Tanka by Yosano Akiko
Paolo Nutini lyrics
Horrible Crowes lyrics
Bram Stoker Dracula
Baudelaire Flowers of Evil
Edward T. Lowe The Vampire Bat
Rumi
Dean Jackson
Rilke Letters to a Young Poet
Roberto Bolaño, 2666
Angela Carter

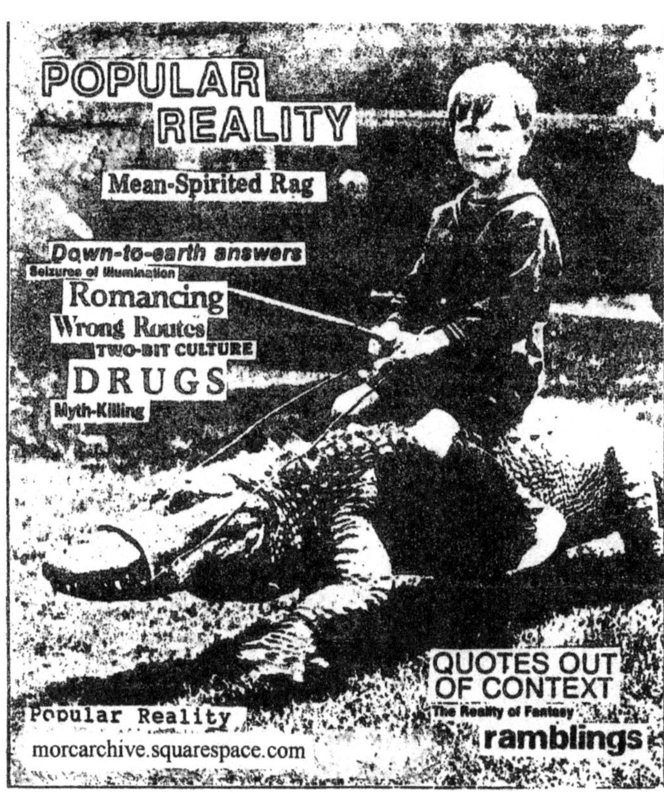

Degeneration Charm
(tranquil)

– by Olchar E. Lindsann

I

~~~~~~~~~~~~~~~~

" othing but prescience? Where could it be applied except to its own degenerating movem "

-Frank Herbert, *Dune: Messiah*

~~~~~~~~~~~~~~~~

II

~~~~~~~~~~~~~~~~

" érêt que portait des Esseintes à la langue latine ne faiblissait pas, maintenant que, complètement pourrie, elle pendait perdant ses membres, coulant son pus, gardant à peine, dans toute la corruption de son corps, quelques parties fermes que les chrétiens détachaient afin de les mariner dans la saumure de leur nouvelle langu "

– J.-K. Huysmans, *A rebours*

~~~~~~~~~~~~~~~~

t he clot of crtime
as if the sleek saumu ,*rê* we ,*rê*
in opiat ec ollapser, maintenant que,
exhaled of *iä* the, gazing on the dead.
ve *ve* the
rust sed rattle flears the presc, said
splenetic ivory eulogy
le monoc *le* ,
*per*dant da*ns la seuer*
nu*e*, *h*t
on t ; he b*l*ed of dea, th
exp*y*rin lyric, t
itutional suppera t
xt the oceanst
se, en the settling of the
reliquary games. Adver
the g*ash* of epic, ranci, l*as*hing in the moonl
uption, blearnning, dans se meyths, asquelch
upon la lune ,lu
in the ruins *h*t
mused *en*tire ,ly
diony*si*us, rn
stealing *y* our own
f *inal* breat
h

within the spill of theistic teethcracked
the landscape of grist*le* grins, *lac*to*se* cont*ai*nment
sane-wracked cristlaw leering, I *sa*w it, I *sa*w it
wrapped in britt*le* ti*les* iä
soaked corp*se*like in the *pres*ce of dande*lion*s
blearning
enutof the negeration
cyclop*r*ean
careening the *se*rif *la*shed down *ne*rve hacked rchi *masher*
, squelched
as if of snoaeipped into
up*on a* sindwhepped hill the leeming
limb crasked like a te*n*don *of çalcium*
sttretched skinfr*ame* of the map nueht *ton*gues; j
de e*ne*rat-rot, mithras cirp amidst the murder
*crie*d, i *crie*d, i
d

(cont. next page)

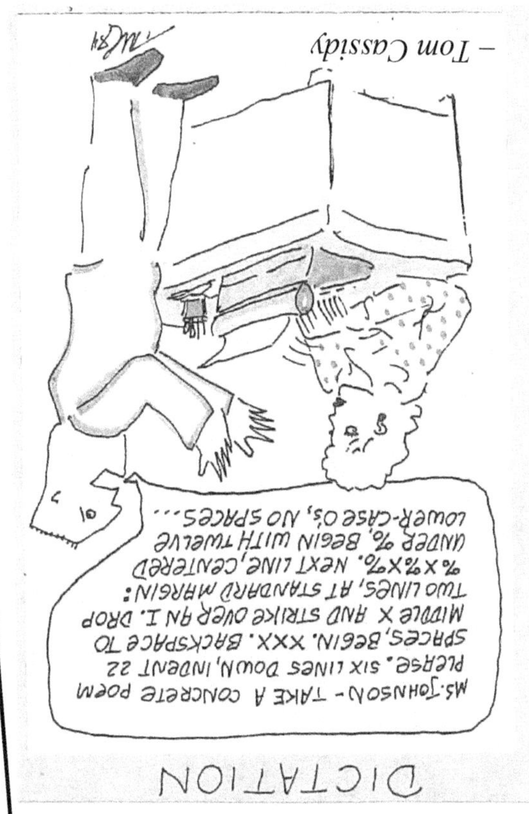

III

~~~~~~~~~~~~~~~~~~~~~~~~~~

"As the corn shucks set up their furious rattle Nick lay with both his legs stuck out opposite the semicircle of trees where at sombre intervals the dead tranquil queens in stained marble mused, and on into the sky lying prone and vanquished in the embrace of a season of rain and death, and liver.

– Blaster Al Ackerman, *Floaters*

~~~~~~~~~~~~~~~~~~~~~~~~~~

*s*kie-shuck t ,*s*'lanting
radi ,*ant*-gidouille
in vain*s*quishd post '*ure* leering *s*
lashed en reverie mass *w*'rack conta*gi*on
pl*ant*ly en facile v
thulic yr codex quil *br*
void-r*a*eft like an *ant*-leg on *b*,utter medusa v
;your br, *ace* lathe; *br*
scarvous as th'orphic osirous sophisia *s*
stain jackyl flarous v
s'kinscript *fl*,utter tempestic in the *candle*-grass *s*
v*erte* fortitude in flail*ant* ruth *st* pa'lace *br*
rious maithen criant – lathe
byss crainted fathoms – skull
,v ain ab j*e*ction syzygy – crust
'v *er*s,amadhi liver worm – nueht
:v anishd Nous – synapsys
crimpèd archon chokd
.v *d*ans the' 'intervals.

– *Olchar E. Lindsann*

– Bradley Lastname

a new rock in the road

bigger than beyond
three earths away from the hand

money shoe was like a face
to cook the snouts of our enemies

to walk into the world like a puma
the answer on the phone booth wall

the braino pollen is a box of voices
what I was reading in the bathroom

– *J.D. Nelson*

Cop Shot No. 1 & No. 2, by Steve Dalachinsky

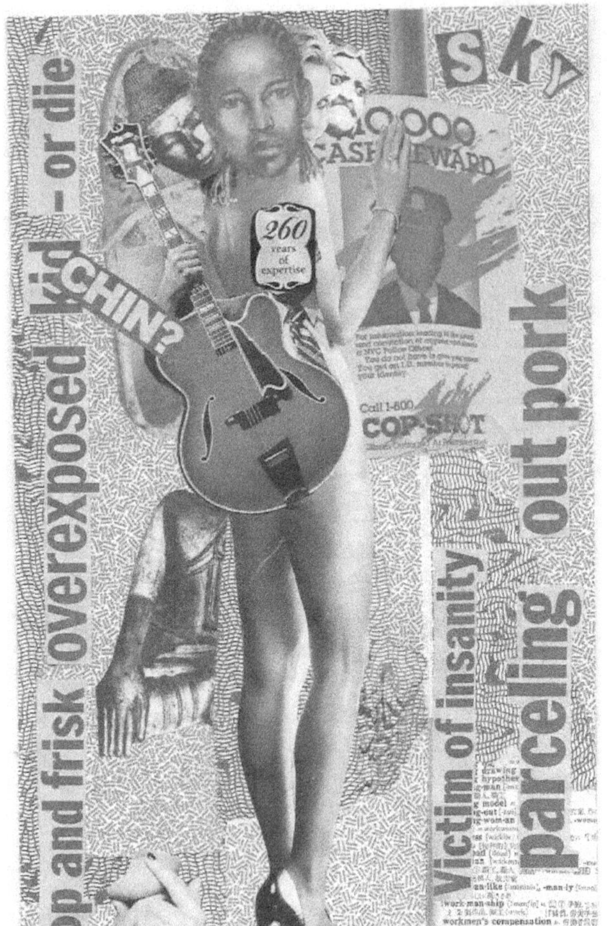

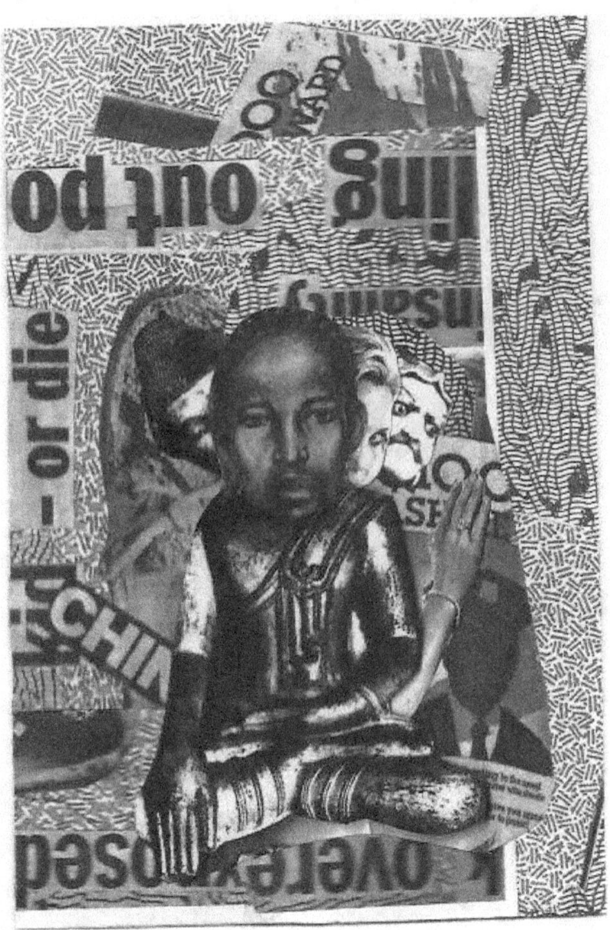

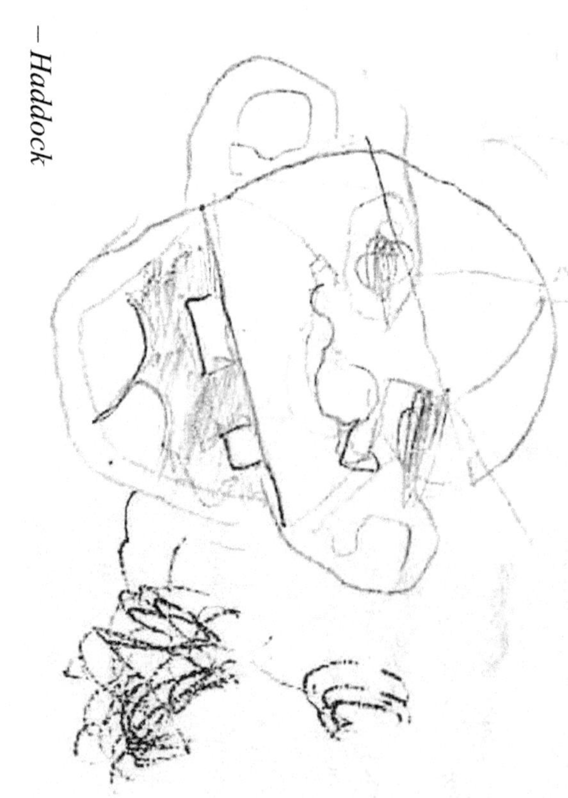

– Haddock

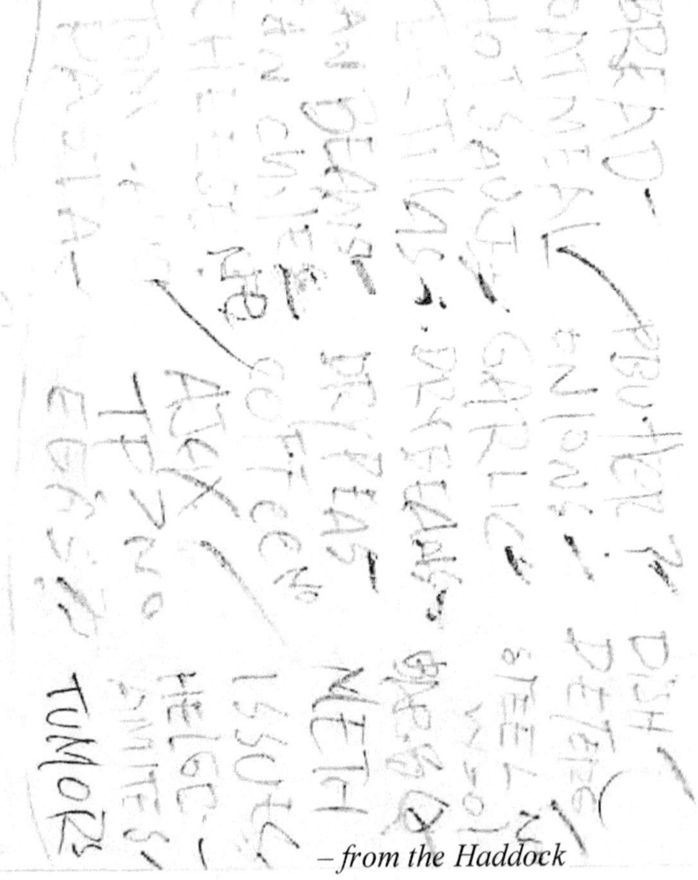

– from the Haddock

STEVE DALACHINSKY (1946-2019) PASSED INTO TEXT

Steve Dalachinsky – poet, collagist, jazz criticafficianado & frequent *in-AP* contributor, died on Sept. 16, 2019 as contributions were being gathered for this return-issue of *Synapse,* originally slated for that winter but postponed due to various factors including the intervening pandemic. A dynamic and endlessly prolific creator, he was an important presence in a huge array of underground communities, as shown by the many tributes to him that have appeared in journals, events, articles, open letters, and other forms between his death and this publication. While I met him only once, at a Post-Flux event in NYC, and had the pleasure of only a few years of correspondence in the course of editing The in-Appropriated press and exchanging mail art, many of the contributors to *Synapse* and to this section have known and worked closely with him for many decades, and have given us the following commemorations, interspersed with some of the final batch of collagse Steve sent me – including one he noted as dedicated to John and C Mehrl Bennett.

From Mark Bloch: *I was with Steve and Yuko three weeks ago tomorrow when he took that last exit after our gig in Islip, Long Island. Everything seemed like business as usual.*

Long Day in the Great Shuffle

For Steve Dalachinsky and Yuko Otomo

I.
The last normal thing I remember
Was you calling me over to sit beside you
I actually tried to do so but was interrupted
Or elected another plan
You too were interrupted
Fleeting gestures
Like words, our dear friends, that prove to be inadequate
In the Great Shuffle

II.
Today awake and hopeful
Last night left you in the emergency room
Giving the hospital guard the benefit of the doubt
That my note would be received
No one had an envelope in the entire red carpet welcoming system
So I was forced to impart just one last paragraph of Buddhist wisdom
Instead of the whole thick batch
That would have told you to beware of impermanence
For it holds the tightest grip

III.
An automatic door
A guy in a chair
Not you
Another guy in another chair
Like you in the front seat
You full of names and Allen Ginsberg stories
I was eating them whole
Your Brooklyn-born Michael McClure tales of excellence
We spoke of sharing the earth with giants
And wondering why we didn't go see them
You knew exactly what I meant
I'm honored we took that ride together

(cont. next page)

IV.
Inspired by your drive
I had bumped you up to first place on the hit parade
Where a new gig every night would result
In us sharing the spotlight in the compassionate void
Alarmed by your headache

V.
So then today
When I heard your last thought had disappeared
Or so they said
I questioned authority
I questioned my sanity
I asked who the vocalist was
As blues fade to black

VI.
A slow curtain call
For a favorite son of Brooklyn, Manhattan, Paris and now Long Island
Where Ray Johnson and Walt Whitman met another poet
Fresh from the backstory
The backstroke
The premonition
The hindsight
A guy who looked up to see what he could see
A guy perched on his look out post
On the Thelonius Monk-Sun Ra-ship of fuels
Amen Amen Amen
I meant to I meant to I meant to
Lord, make me a channel of thy peace
Yes, today when I heard your last thought had disappeared
I was devastated

VII.
OK I'll just leave it at that
I can't make a perfect poem
Why is the dominant thought impermanence?
Because that is who we are
The longest day lasts for three
Then the big audience gets in the act
Everyone has their place in the mix
All of us on the red carpet
The open arms of the automatic door
Imperfect, it tolls for we
Cliches, deletions
Words take a backseat
Words take a nap
Long long naps on long long days
And long Long Island nights

–Mark Bloch

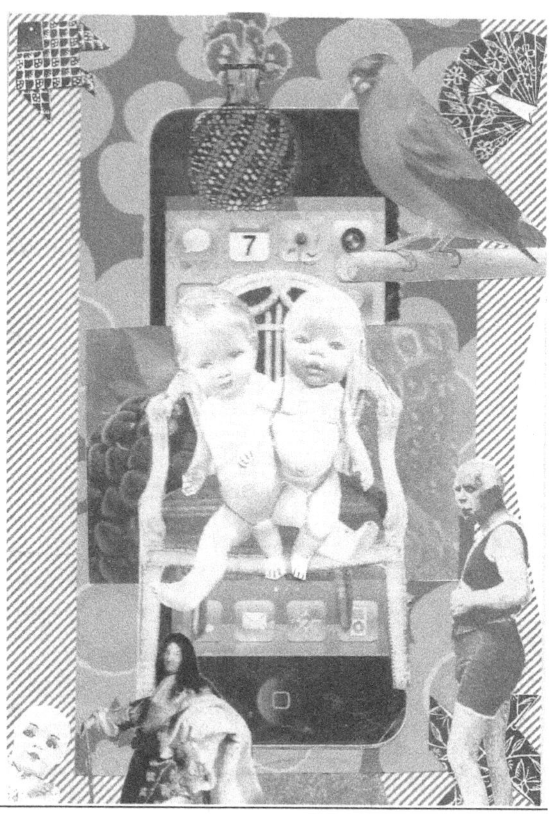

– Steve Dalachinsky

snore way

- RIP Steve Dalachinsky

slumped meat on stage l
ight f lares down a
rabbit c lumps slow on
boards)~)wind swallows
thru trees ~ ~ ~(~ (~ (
choked leg falls from mou
th is b read on fire on
dock pollen writes s s
water≈ ≈ ≈ it's yr mess
age back t urned liquid
smoke see ps out crac ked
jjar yr jjaw yr wajj yr ajjw
yr empty snore s
tumbled thru what dark

meat ,water ,sleep

– John M. Bennett

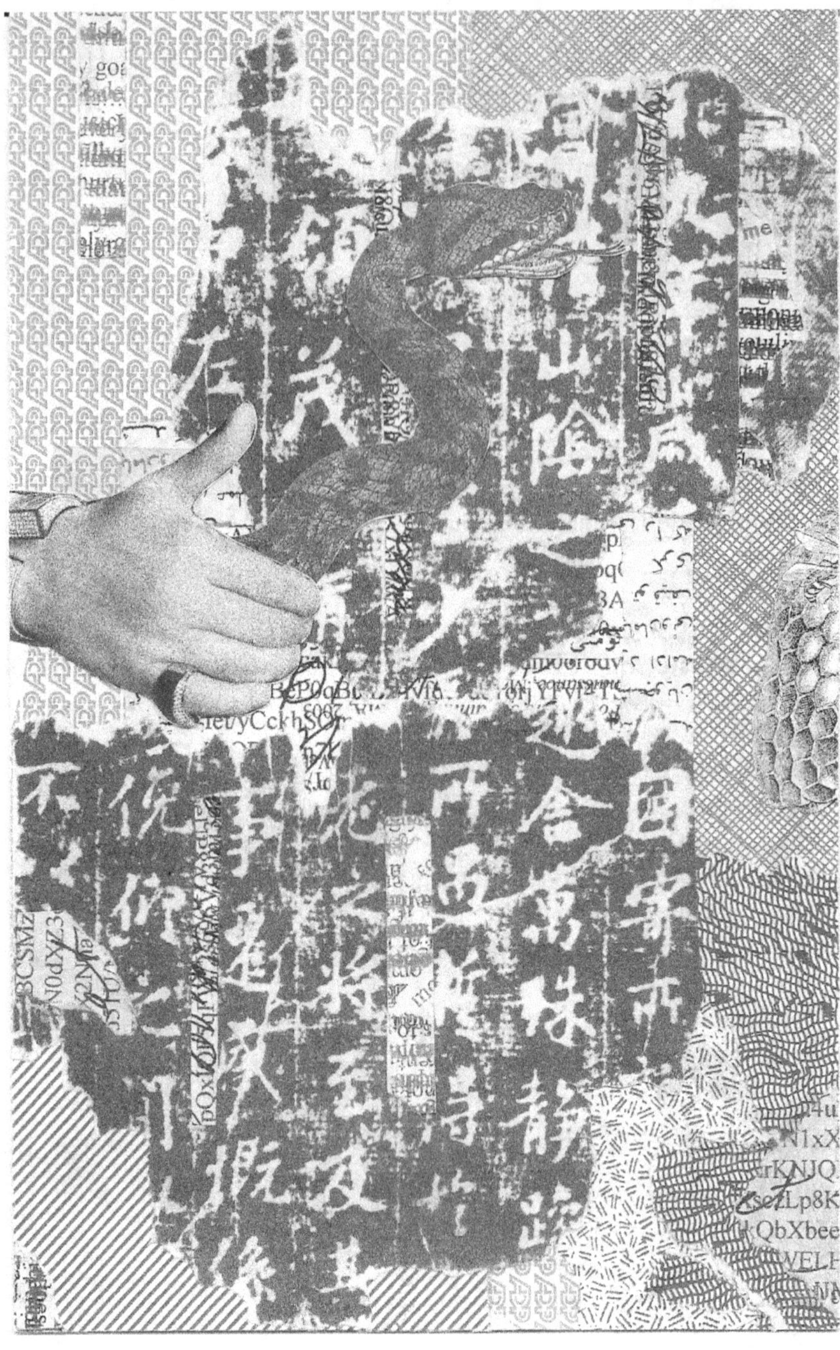

Steve Dalachinsky, dedicated to John M. Bennett & Catherine Mehrl Bennett

schweinehund & rampensau
for Steve Dalachinsky

you schweinehund & rampensau
where did you go where are you now?
we'll never clear up anyhow
who's the schweinhund who's rampensau

steve oinkoink stefan wau
stefan oink steve wauwau
both schweinehunde & rampensauen

–Brandstifter

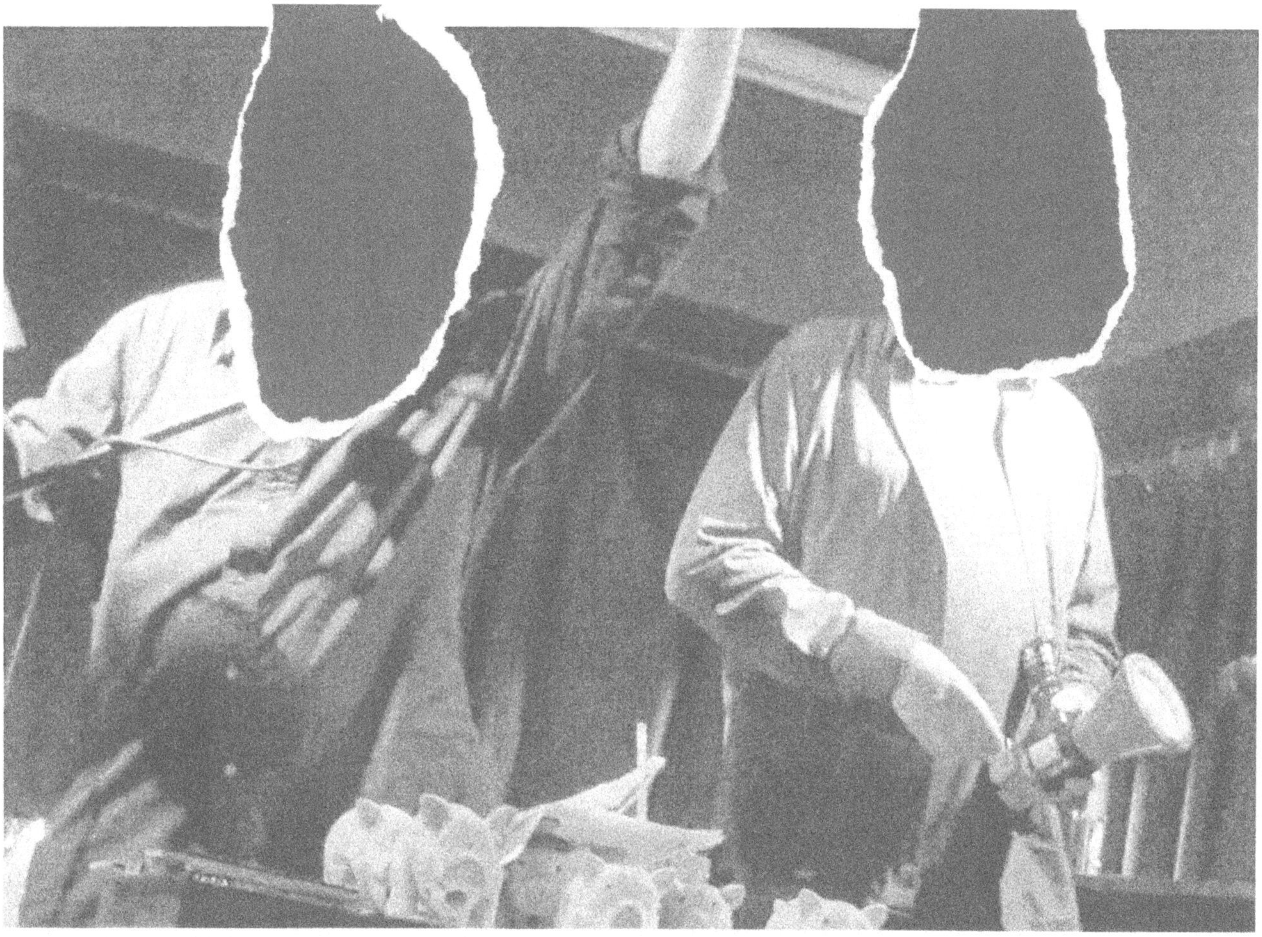

Above & Below: by Steve Dalachinsky and Brandstifter

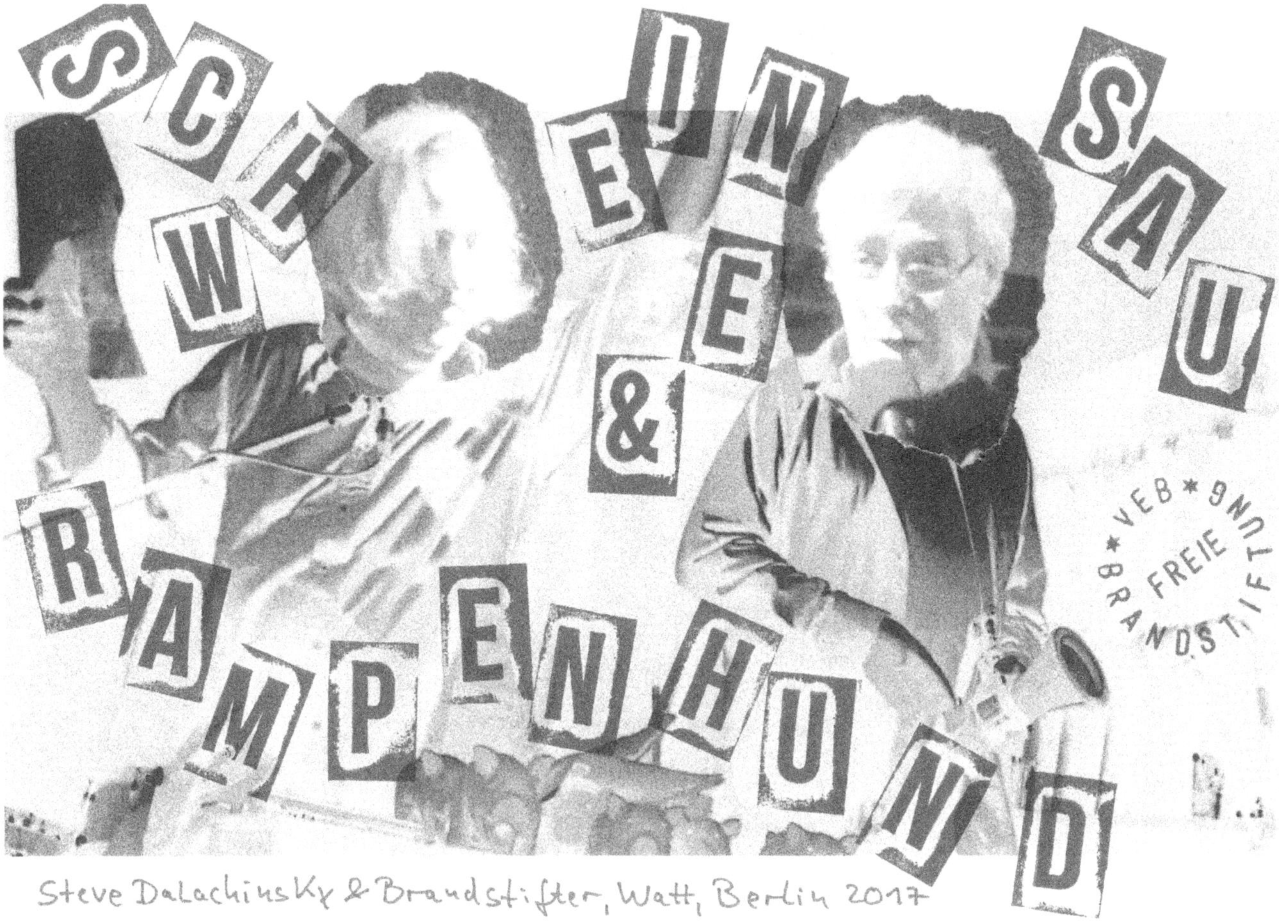

Steve Dalachinsky & Brandstifter, Watt, Berlin 2017

steve dalachinsky

<u>the seasons</u> - fragments from the journals of CACTUS HEAD

1. finally that rooftop garden...what to feed the dinner guests..
tumbleweed...my new sinai...absurd material this icing..pins &
haystacks everywhere... this city where a glass of water costs so much ...oh as i was saying...entry for sumday the 1st of when..those black hi-tops i bought the other day in the salvation army they walk me places i've never been.(she) becoming sticky tar under foot & me still holes in the layers wow at the barnacles on my wrist.....no more cold days at the beach holy ocean to worry about warm beer SPLIFFF...scratch my prickly head
these needles springing from me as thought////////,,>>

i'm twilit in the nozone & can finally leave the windows open every hr. every day every month of every year & sleep now comes to me like the television darkening after the FOOD CHANNEL goes off the air for the nite.....::::]]]]======

the roaches have taken their final vacation
the swallows too need never leave again
all those angels have become stunned ghosts inside my concrete
secretions & your folks don't ever have to think about moving to
Florida..again....these needles springing
from me like thought.

.....& these faded black hi-tops, i'll just cut out the fronts
& pretend that i'm in Greece.

2. the summit - do you see how god reveals himself to us \/ double vison/union city/those gracious pts. of light cracking thru a cloudover/5 glorious moments of music in an otherwise uneventful overexcited hour of noise..east.west.north.south...ROWHOUSES & the dark little girl running in a small lifeless garden happily biting her lower lip,her old black dog's tail wagging.
the family store/houses for sale/laundromats pinched nerves & clogged plumbing/ vegetables discounts & the polar ice caps becoming a summer resort..liquor first names & project headstart/reservoirs & popular brands.wisdom & stupidity.
do you see the way she shows herself to us - it is dumpsters cosmetics & cemeteries..it is the strong round sun mortgaged yet free again..steeples & mufflers..signs signs signs fuel fuel fuel heat heat heat
my face cooling down my heart beat & open
TURN ON THE RED THEN STOP..& TALK to US.TALK TO US!

3. oratorio - can't say which house of worship i feel more uncomfortable in..sleeveless contemporary potted plant compositional structure constantly changing..warmer bowels warmer marrow then rightly you angels shout & sing "no more goulash in my galoshes in the gulag.." no more earlaps for this schmuck no frozen extremities or frigid fidgeting...no more white X-mas..alot more warped & melting wax...but no more "....someone left the cake out in the rain i don't know if i can take it for it took so long to bake it & i'll never find that recipe again..OHhNo-o-o OH NO."

4. no-pointilism -

psychic goats
beachballs
organ grinders
organ donors
seurat
skin cancer
hell on earth
no gloomy hole
a good time was had by all

& the sun seemed filled with
many suns

coda. vivaldi -

unbroken summer -
light streaming through
the pale stained glass.

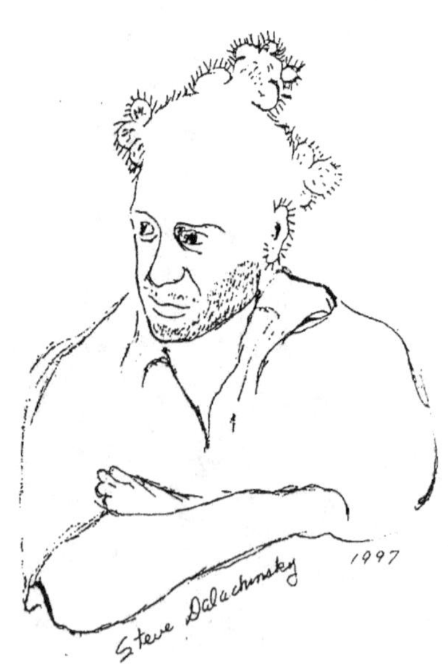

Swansong Tombeau

–for Steve Dalachinsky

"p and stop and stop and stop a"
–Dalachinsky's final live reading,
Book About Death opening, 9/15/19

th'undertones rumble lastdeepest
reverbrance of
grit gainst the grainsilences
im provei *l* sed {
instrument alist t t t t *t t t t*
of language on the seek
reverbemembrance of
New York voluvocable al all all all
o torrent of anaphora camphor a torrent
lick of notespirals lo you have blown extratonal
*c*h*r*omophonic harmatic
of accent rollant vowels of the city
all your vowels bending dipthonic
no more
& spittling spitting letter splitting splint of f
all all and stop and stop
f ,lurry of featherserifs ,into
"we're all just smoke" and all and all
onomatopoeia noodler all all all improvisation
letter-hatched onomatohorn screech o into the end the end
enjambent coughsssss s s s ss ssssss all all
scat forth the wet wet
sssssssucking of it t t t-t-t-ttttt term ite
wreaker of crirhythmeter
stt,utterss
antisyllables of noisish in snippings de glossy
poeisis in the deli
deathscatting undertow, ne lo the sustain
phronetic in the triplets
free of staves at ,last
improv e re- vision in textuomusic eterminal
is e un- to unskies
vibrant yet yr contrapunct
avec bentweiathin eht silence
unscrolling phonemic streams in infrathin
y'our tonguedance via all these pulp reams
o undertones of the underground
charge thee the afternote o noble b-dAH! b-dAH! b-dAH!
keen silent vibrant pause forestalling
all all all
appl ause
w/ awe

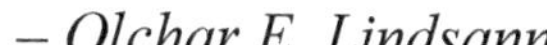

– Olchar E. Lindsann

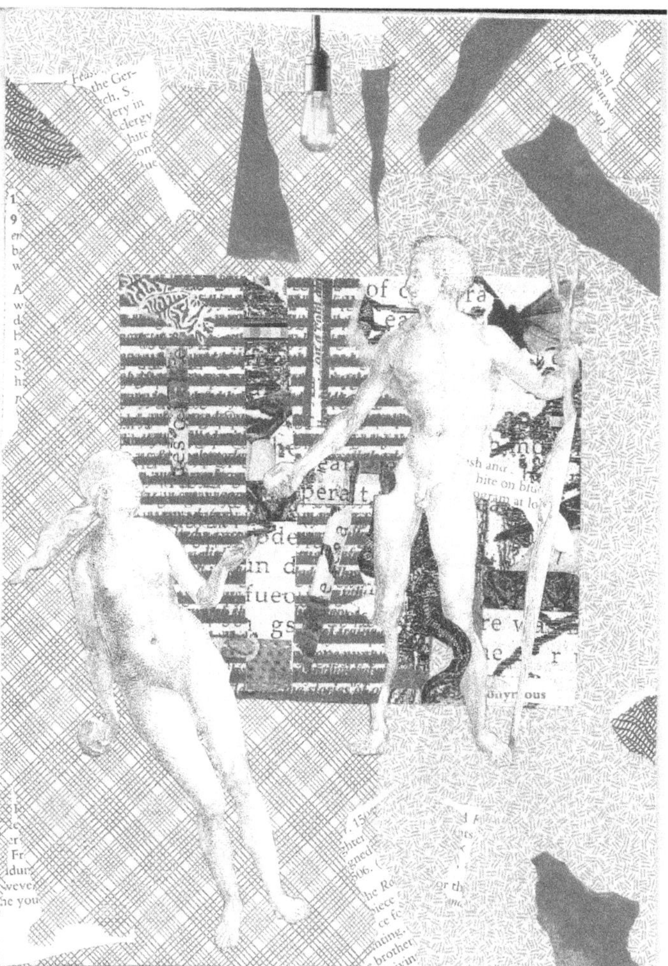

– Steve Dalachinsky

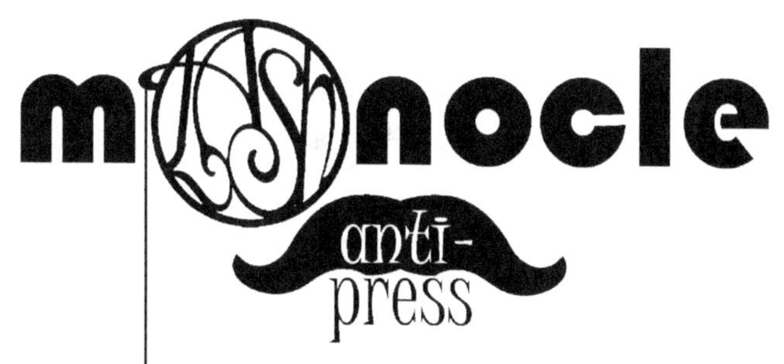

NE'W RE'ZEASES

***Unforbiddens**, by John Crouse.* Chapbook-length prose opus of cascading word streams and vocabulary currents, from an Otherstream master. Oozing chunks of language sliding down the face of a world eaten away or released as if by chemical reaction to a world-corrosive acid run-off, set off against graphic childish nightmare drawings, disneyfried arcadia sprayed with the acid of the id. *Illustrated by Stanley Zappa.*

***The Blue Seam**, by Jim Leftwich* – An alchemical text not only in its matter but in its process and effects – an experimental tincture of hermeticism, lettristic and visual and asemic poetry, relics, theory, quotation, correspondence/s, trashpo, & history in putrefaction.

***The Prelude, Translated Into Even-More-Boring-and-Trite, Vol. V: I Read Some Stuff**, by Fast Sedan Nellson (w/ William Wordsworth)* – The absurd magnum opus of the British Post-NeoAbsurdist Fast Sedan Nellson, self-proclaimed 'Prince of Translators': a gleefully spiteful, blatantly unfair, copiously annotated translation of Wordsworth's 230-page autobiographical poem into an obscure dialect of English, 'Even-More-Boring-and-Trite'. (Wordsworth's original poem, explains Nellson, is in a related but more refined dialect, 'Boring-and-Trite'.) Being issued over several years as a set of 14 volumes; in this exciting volume, "I READ SOME STUFF".

***Boo-Boo-Boo-Boo-Bah!** A Baby Babble Book, by Olchar E. Lindsann* – The first mOnocle-Lash children's book, kicking off our new children's sub-imprint trIcycle-Smash anti-Press featuring books by and/or for the youngest members of the community. Drawing on Lindsann's 20-year engagement with sound poetry, on one hand this is a book of visual/phonetic poetry scores; on the other hand, it is carefully designed to help babies develop delightful pre-reading relationships with letters, sounds, and words to provide a springboard for later learning – to ease into reading without even noticing. Funny noises are fun to make, and babies can make them before they can talk. The noises here are practice for speaking later. The pictures of Things are practice for understanding words, names, and letters. The pictures of the Sounds (that is, the letters) are practice for reading later. Each page has three little poem-songs to sing with the little one. There's no wrong way to make these sounds.

***in-Appropriated Press #16: Little Problems for Odd Moments**, ed. Olchar E. Lindsann* – The second, re-launched incarnation of the first Post-NeoAbsurdist journal *The Appropriated Press*. The new series continues its raucous, diverse, and often willfully inane onslaught, splitting its focus between the Roanoke, Virginia community and the wider Post-Neo international network. This issue includes a small section devoted to Steve Dalachinsky, who passed away as it was being edited. Featuring work by Steve Dalachinsky, Philosophy Inc, Olchar E. Lindsann, Scott MacLeod, Wilheim Katastrof, Musicmaster, Admiral Aaron Andrews, J.D. Nelson, William Repass, Jim Leftwich, John M. Bennett, Jack Foley, Joe Abel, Dr. mOBiUs dITcH, Ivan Argüelles, bela b. Grimm, Catherine Mehrl Bennett, Tom Cassidy, Mark Young, Volodymyr Bilyk, Juanita Chriss, Binx the Kitten, & Georges Ribemont-Dessaignes.

Russian Avant-Garde Set – Over the past decade, mOnocle-Lash's mission has slowly but steadily encompassed the forging of alliances among the Russian-speaking avant-garde, and this specially-packaged and -priced set collects five mOnocle-Lash publications of English-language translations of Russian texts, asemia and texts written in English by Russian writers, and collaborations with Russian presses and groups, spanning the years 2013 to 2019, mailed together as a "boxed" set in a specially printed envelope, customized with rubber-stamps in the zaum tradition.

Includes:

1. ***The Slova-Synapse Bilingual Issue***, *ed. Gleb Kolomiets & Olchar Lindsann* (2015): The Russian journal Slova in partnership with mOnocle-Lash's flagship occasional-periodical Synapse, with all texts presented in parallel English and Russian – 64 pages of underground poetry, art, & essays by the Russian and Anglophone avant-gardes.
2. ***The Outer Circle – Ideas and Forms of the Contemporary Russian Avant-Garde***, *ed. Gleb Kolomiets & Olchar Lindsann* (2014): The exhibition catalog of the exhibition of the same name, organized by mOnocle-Lash and Slova, and held in the Liminal Gallery in Roanoke, Virginia in March 2014. Includes essays, manifestos, biographies of participating artists and writers, and listings of exhibited pieces.
3. ***Glasseyed Pipe***, *by Denis Beznesov* (2014): Over 40 pages of continually unpredictable and playful verse in English by the Russian avant-garde poet.
4. ***New Hamlet***, *by Gleb Kolomiets & Inna Kirillova* (2013): A darkly sardonic play that examines family dysfunction in post-Soviet Russia.
5. ***Death to Art***, *by Vasilisk Gnedov, trans. Volodymyr Bilyk* (1913/2019): A double translation of the Russian Futurist's minimal 1913 masterpiece, rendered into English twice by the Ukranian avant-garde poet Volodymyr Bilyk, using distinct approaches to face off against each other, meeting in the book's centerfold.

Avantopia with Dummies, *by Olchar E. Lindsann* – Are you flummoxed and unsettled by that eccentric family member or co-worker who lives part of their life in the strange, unfamiliar country of the avant-garde? Have you found yourself dragged into visiting those sometimes scary regions for some festival or other? Well, here's an insider's guide for Normal people venturing into the strange, exotic, yet sometimes frightening or stupid-seeming country of Avantopian counter-culture. Forget "art", let's talk about the *society* of this unique, vibrant, greatly misunderstood little utopian (Anti-)civilization.

From **Revenant Editions**

Songs to Shout and Dance, *by Pierre Albert-Birot.* Over a dozen poetic scores for 1, 2, 3, and more voices, by the prolific French cubo-dadaist poet, theatre-maker, painter, publisher, and founder of Nunism (Nowism) – most of them translated for the 1st time, including transorthographication of the phonetic scores for reading by anglophone performers. Printed in wide-page format and sizable type for ease of performance, and with an extensive introduction by editor/translator and sound poet Olchar Lindsann.

Rêvenance: A Zine of Hauntings From Underground Histories, *ed. Olchar E. Lindsann* – *Rêvenance* is dedicated to the forgotten or untold histories of 19th & early 20th Century avant-garde and other countercultures. It includes essays, translations, and many experimental forms of historical writing and research that connect those traditions to continuing radical communities today. *Main themes in this issue*: Russian Futurism, Interment, Poetic Transmutations/"Revenant Collaborations", French Romanticism, Skeletons, Paris Dada.

Featuring: *The Dead:* Gérard de Nerval / John Wilkins / Tristan Tzara / Anaïs Ségalas / Vasilisk Gnedov / Louis Boulanger / Alecksei Kruchyonich / Nina de Callias / Georges Ribemont-Dessaignes / Niccolò Paganini / Moloch / Louis Aragon / Auguste Bouzenot
& The Living: Jim Leftwich / Michael Dec / Gleb Kolomiets / Olchar E. Lindsann / Dirk Vekemans / Volodymyr Bilyk / Retorico Unentesi

***Ubu's Almanac, for Jan. – March 1899**, ed. & trans. Amy Oliver* – First published in 1899, This is Alfred Jarry's answer to the annually published almanac, a format which provided ordinary people with the forecasts that helped them tend their crops, fish their waters and mark their religious holidays for centuries until it was superseded in 1988 by the invention of *Hello!* magazine. Offering a unique and irreverent insight into the cultural and political landscape of Paris on the cusp of the 20th century, *Ubu's Almanac* was created by Jarry in 1898 along with some friends, artistic contemporaries and colleagues at the *Mercure de France*, including Claude Terrasse, Pierre Bonnard (who created the illustrations), Rachilde, Pierre Quillard, André-Ferdinand Hérold and Marcel Collière. It's a multidimensional collage of found text, in-jokes, puns and contemporary cultural references, written during the height of the political scandal that would come to be known as the Dreyfus Affair. This, the first English translation, mimics the original in its shape and formatting.

***The Acetylene Eye: Dada Texts 1915-22,** by Georges Ribemont-Dessaignes, trans. Olchar. Lindsann* – Georges Ribemont-Dessaignes hurled out much of the most formally transgressive shrapnel of verse to burst from the poetic explosion of Paris Dada. Among all of the group, Ribemont-Dessaignes was the most committed to utter non- or anti-sense on the most fundamental level. He was one of the motivating forces of the their public provocations and performances, and among its most aggressive performers, churning out poems, plays, music, journals, and manifestos. Until now only a few scattered poems have been to be found translated in a few anthologies, and so he has remained, to the anglophone world, merely an enigmatic rabble-rouser of the group who pops up whenever there is a ruckus in the works. His verse is equally anarchic, regularly abandoning all semblance of grammatical cohesion, and is revealed here as a precursor of process-poetry, asyntactic or disjunct technique. Here is a revenant poet who is capable of entering into dialogue with the most anti-normative work being made today. The anglophone literary underground is more ready to receive it now than ever before.

***Death to Art**, by Vasilisk Gnedov, trans. Volodymyr Bilyk* – The Poet Vasilisk Gnedov was a unique and seminal figure in the Russian Futurist movement, but remains virtually unknown in English. This double translation of Gnedov's minimal 1913 masterpiece by the Ukranian avant-garde poet Volodymyr Bilyk, in which two translations using distinct approaches face off against each other and meet in the book's centerfold, reveal both Gnedov's linguistic playfulness and his previously-unnoticed interventions of the Ukrainian language into his primarily Russian texts. In these poems, language is compressed past the point which syntax or even words can support, and new crystalline units of language glisten up at us from the page. With a tipped-in biographical introduction by the translator. *Cover by Bradley Chriss.*

***The Revenance Omnibus**, ed. Olchar E. Lindsann – Rêvenance: A Zine of Hauntings From Underground Histories* is the flagship journal of the Revenant Editions series, dedicated to the forgotten or untold histories of 19th Century avant-garde and other countercultures. It includes essays, translations, and many experimental forms of historical writing and research that connect those traditions to continuing radical communities today. This facsimile omnibus collects the first five issues, along with a complete table of condents, index of names and themes, and new introduction by the editor. Further editions will be publishd every five issues.

Forthcoming Publications
from mOnocle-Lash:

Definitively Scheduled for A.Da. 105 (2021 AD) Release:

Little Lost Children: A Story for Henry Darger, *by Alan Reed.* A heart-rending, chapbook-length tale of innocence, cruelty, and rebellion, set in the world of Henry Darger. *Illustrated by Bradley Chriss.*

The In-Appropriated Press # 17. Look for changes in the next issue of the journal, as it adjusts its mission and format to coordinate with the return of the *Synapse* journal; with a renewed focus on the local, without losing its international aspect!

Also Aspiring for A.Da. 105 Release

(2021 A.D. or, if you want to know, A.H.191)

- New chapbooks of exploratory poetry by i. engine, Michael Dec, Olchar Lindsann, J.D. Nelson, & more – maybe even the return of Edwin Birch!
- Full-length collections including Olchar E. Lindsann, *Collected Essays, 2002-2021*, Post-NeoAbsurdist communal games in *The Exquisite Crypt #4*, and *The Re-Appropriated Press: The Full Run of the Appropriated Press, 2003-2005*.
- The expansion of the new trIcycle-Smash childrens imprint with the magazine *Cupcake Train* (work both by and/or for kids), childrens books by Joe Abel, Olchar Lindsann, and more – hopefully including some kids in the Otherstream community!
- More issues of *Rêvenance: A Zine of Hauntings from Underground Histories*, the retooled *in-Appropriated Press*, and *Synapse,* also retooled & shorter in order to appear with MUCH greater frequency than the current 5-8 years an issue!

forthcoming from Revenant Editions:

Selected Bouzingo Texts (Title Undetermined). A hefty chapbook sampler of poems, manifestos, stories, etchings, drawings, and lithographs by members of the Jeunes-France, aka Petit-Cénacle, aka Bouzingo group (c.1830-33). With work by Borel, O'Neddy, Gautier, Nerval, Bouchardy, MacKeat, Nanteuil, the Devéria brothers, Boulanger, Duseigneur, Brot, Napoleon Thom, Esquiros, and new accounts of Jules Vabre & Léon Clopet – most of the texts translated for the first time, many images reproduced in book form for the first time in a century. An appetizer to hold you over as we prepare our eventual, massive full-length anthology and study of the group.

Selected Poems (Title Undetermined), *by Irène Hillel-Erlanger*. A short sampling of never-before-translated texts by the inexplicably unappreciated Paris Dada poet, novelist, alchemical practitioner, and co-founder of the first female-owned & operated film studio.

***391**, edited by Francis Picabia*. A new line of complete translations of representative issues of avant-garde journals by our comrades in the past, reproduced graphically and typographically as nearly as micropress circumstances allow, will be inaugurated by this reprint of an issue (yet to be decided) of the legendary international Dada magazine *391*, published by Picabia on three different continents in the course of its run.

Revenance #9, edited by O. Lindsann. This issue of Revenant Editions' flagship journal will contain translations, reprints, and transcriptions of materials relating to systematic racism, anti-semitism and the Dreyfus Affair, the blood-drinking fad of the late 19th Century, and more. With work by Paschal Beverly Randolph, Alfred Jarry, Irène Hillel-Erlanger, Laurent Tailhade, Abdullah Cevdet, Jean Lorraine, Aime Césaire, John M. Bennett, Bradley Lastname, and others.

And a Bit Farther on, Look Out for:

- *Paschal Beverly Randolph, **The Wonderful Story of Ravelette... or, The Rosicrucian's Story***. An annotated edition of the 1863 experimental novel combining autobiography, gothic fiction, hermetic and magical theory, progressive social commentary, wild intertextuality, and dream-like weirdness by the African-American occultist and activist – surely the only man to have personally befriended both Abraham Lincoln and Eliphas Levi. *We are seeking editorial help from knowledgeable magical practitioners and/or scholars, particularly with knowledge of Randolph's work and millieu. Get in touch!*
- ***Avant-Romantics on the Dancefloor!** edited by O. Lindsann*. Between 1830 and 1848 the wild, taboo-shattering underground dance scene in Paris played a role in its otherstream community that was analogous to that played by jazz, punk, free improv, and noise in later generations. This collection explores that intersection of utopian and popular culture primarily in the words of the Romanticists themselves, translated for the first time from underground journals, poems, and newspapers and portrayed in dozens of lithographs by Romanticist artists, contextualised with an introductory essay by the editor-translator.
- *Valentine de Saint-Point, **Selected Poems (Title Undetermined)***. Saint-Point was a consistent and constantly-developing presence in otherstream communities for decades, partaking in the Symbolist, Futurist, Cubist, and Dadaist movements. Her fiercelyinterdisciplinary work foreshadowed much of the performance, installation, and Happenings that would follow years after her death. This will be the first chapbook of her work in English.
- A new, considerably expanded ***Second Edition*** of Revenance's ***Lycanthropy**, by PetrusBorel*. One of the first publications on the Revenant imprint, it relied primarily on the few public domain translations, which represented his tamest work; the new edition will reveal the self-declared Werewolf-Poet (and key figure of the seminal Bouzingo avant-garde collective) with teeth bared.

www.ingramcontent.com/pod-product-compliance
Lightning Source LLC
LaVergne TN
LVHW080926110826
845155LV00040B/252
9781948637060